FOREST FRINGE
The First Ten Years

CONTENTS

Part I – Introductory texts

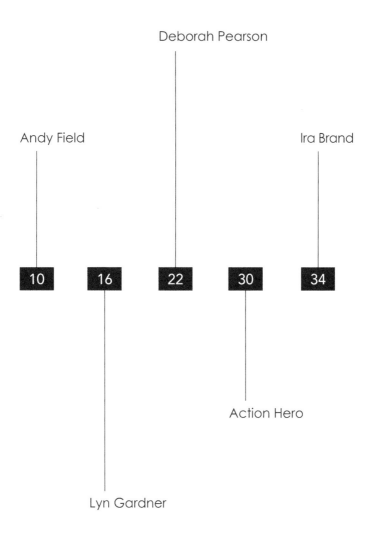

Part II – Documents of Forest Fringe

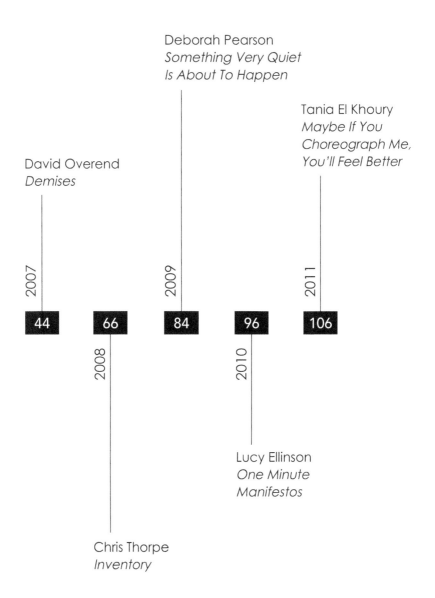

Deborah Pearson
*Something Very Quiet
Is About To Happen*

Tania El Khoury
*Maybe If You
Choreograph Me,
You'll Feel Better*

David Overend
Demises

2007

2009

2011

| 44 | 66 | 84 | 96 | 106 |

2008

2010

Lucy Ellinson
*One Minute
Manifestos*

Chris Thorpe
Inventory

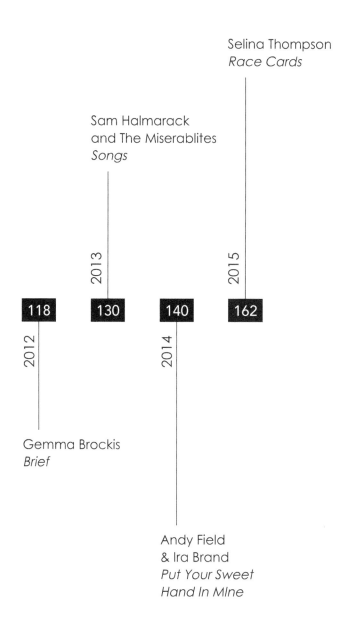

Selina Thompson
Race Cards

Sam Halmarack
and The Miserablites
Songs

2013

2015

118   130   140   162

2012   2014

Gemma Brockis
Brief

Andy Field
& Ira Brand
*Put Your Sweet
Hand In Mine*

PART – I

Introductory
—   texts

Andy Field

[Originally published in The Scotsman, August 2013]

Both Forest Fringe and the global financial crisis were born in August 2007. This is just a coincidence. There is no evidence to suggest that one caused the other.

I am thirty years old.
I remember the end
of the Cold War and
Maggie Thatcher
leaving parliament
as images, not as
events. I grew up
in a small village
in the Fens in the
warm glow of the
prosperous 90s.

Capitalism it seemed wasn't just the only game in town,
it was an awesome game, like *Hungry Hungry Hippos*.

The financial
crisis was an event
unlike any that
my generation
had experienced
and it changed
my relationship
to politics, to
capitalism and
to society. While
it may not have
been caused by the
financial crisis,

Forest Fringe has grown up with it and been shaped by it – it has been a place where we, as artists and as a venue, have collectively tried to figure out our relationship to a changing world.

In our earlier years I think this found its embodiment in a politics and an aesthetics of 'making-do'. We made a virtue of meagre circumstances and we compensated for having very little money with what we hoped was an enormous amount of charm. We made cardboard props and hand-painted signs. We used any chairs we could find and hoped people wouldn't mind the dust, or the quietly lingering smell of last night's spilt beer. We used all the lights we could and when those lights blew we improvised by candlelight until we could get to the fuse box. We slept on sofas, and between sofas and in corridors and occasionally in vans. We treasured the poverty of our resources like a wayward best friend; like Dean Moriarty.

These adventures in low-fi manifested themselves in shows with an intimate, amateur aesthetic that was at once humorously self-deprecating and charged with a defiant, radical energy. We celebrated the scrappiness of our victories and the honesty of our failures.

It felt like we had found a language that allowed us to still tell the biggest stories and make them feel like they could still belong to us. A duo called Action Hero made a show called *Watch Me Fall* in which they recreated Evel Knievel's Caesar Palace motorcycle jump with a small red bike, two bottles of diet coke and a pack of Mentos. A company called Paper Cinema used a camcorder and a projector to transform dozens of intricate hand-drawn illustrations into an epic, impossibly beautiful animated film. And another company called Tinned Fingers imagined time travel using only a table lamp and a colander.

It didn't matter that there wasn't any money because we didn't need any, we could find our own alternative way of making things happen. And that self-reliance, that eschewal of the conventional means of production, meant that what we were doing was deeply political, even when all we were doing was daredevil stunts or dancing to *Time After Time*. In the shadow of the failure of the banking industry we were scratching around for a way of doing things that celebrated smallness rather than growth, that recognised that resources are always finite, that to the best of its abilities refused to participate in the unrelenting carnival of late capitalism. And we weren't too worried about being taken all that seriously when it was clear that our most powerful institutions were themselves such a harrowing joke.

As we've got older I think we've perhaps started to push at the limits of always just making do. We have wanted more lights and better sound. We have wanted to free ourselves from the spectre of whimsy, to try on different kinds of voices and see how we sound in them. We have wanted to be able to look after each other better, some of us have children and some of us have mortgages and for whatever reason sleeping on the floor seems to hurt more these days.

Rather than always just making do, we have wanted to find ways of doing things that we couldn't have done before, but we have sought to do so without sacrificing the things that made Forest Fringe good in the first place. Most importantly we are still finding our own alternative means of production, we're still interested in celebrating smallness and independence, in resisting the idea that success is tied to growth, in recognising that resources are finite and growing ever-more so all the time, and we still believe that owning your own venue or your own office or even your own photocopier does not have to be the logistical progression of theatre company like Forest Fringe. What has changed perhaps is that whereas a few years ago we celebrated making the most of the very little we had, now we devote most of our energy and imagination to figuring out how we can make bigger things happen with the help of other people's resources.

Maybe the best example of this is our new festival home at the Out of the Blue Drill Hall on Leith Walk – a huge, beautiful space much loved by the people that use it all year round. Instead of taking over the space we try and share it with the people that already call it home, by finding ways to work around the use they make of the building, and by inviting companies based in the building to be part of the Forest Fringe programme. By sharing the space in this way we can make big, amazing things happen for a fraction of the amount it would have cost if we wanted to occupy the building outright.

We're eight years old now and we're still not a proper organisation. We don't have an office, or salaries, we don't even have a photocopier. But we've put on Forest Fringe festivals for thousands of people in ten different countries and this year's Edinburgh programme is maybe the most diverse, unpredictable, loud and elaborate we've ever had. We haven't really got much bigger, but we've learnt not just to make the best of what we have but the best of what other people have as well. We're still not that concerned about looking professional and many people probably still don't take us that seriously, but perhaps more do than used to.

Lyn Gardner

"YOU MUST COME AND SEE THIS," says a young woman, her eyes shining. How could I possibly refuse such an invitation?

She takes my hand and pulls me up the worn stairs of an old church hall on Bristo Place in Edinburgh. She is determined not going to take no for an answer. This turns out to be an unshowy, generous and wise show called Hitch made by a young Scottish theatre-maker called Kieran Hurley telling of how he hitched his way to the G8 meeting in Aquila in Italy and all those who gave him a helping hand along the way whenever he felt lost.

The room is already crammed, but rather than protecting their personal space people shuffle up to make more room to let us and others sit as if the spirit of the yet to be seen show has already somehow entered the performance area.

For me and for many theatre-goers Forest Fringe has become the oasis on the Edinburgh Fringe, one that puts out a helping hand, pulls you in and makes you take notice of theatre makers who you might otherwise might never have encountered. It was Forest Fringe that offered me my first glimpses of Action Hero, Gary McNair, Peter McMaster, Brian Lobel, Jo Bannon, Emma Frankland, Tania El Khoury, Deborah Pearson, Paper Cinema, Verity Standen and many more. It is Forest Fringe which has sent me on adventures across Edinburgh streets and landscapes, changing my relationship with the city, making me look at it through fresh eyes.

I've come to trust that outstretched hand and the voice urgently saying: **"YOU MUST SEE THIS."** It has led me to see Action Hero shooting down the myths of the wild west in *A Western*, taken me up on Calton Hill for Greg Wohead's *Hurtling*, made me daily check up on the progress of James Baker as he attempted to walk 50 miles into space using only a step ladder over the duration of the Fringe, made me watch open-mouthed as audiences queued up to have the banknotes in their pockets shredded in Gary McNair's *Crunch*, or had Harry Giles tot up my debts—emotional as well as financial. Many of my best Forest Fringe moments have been small and fragile, interventions that have only lasted a few minutes and which are a kind of Tardis theatre: bigger on the inside than they appear from without. Many have required me to be an active participant in the proceedings, not just a spectator.

Forest Fringe may be best known as a place or space in Edinburgh, initially set-up in Bristo Square above a vegan café and more latterly existing for two weeks during the Fringe at the Out of the Blue Drill Hall in Leith.

But it has toured all over the world too, popping-up in unexpected places, and it exists through digital projects, and in some cases via shows that only really exist in the imagination.

I prefer to think of it not as a place but a state of mind, one which has challenged the traditional way that theatre and performance is programmed presented and sold since Deborah Pearson and Andy Field came together and wondered what an artist-led intervention on the Edinburgh Fringe might look like and how it might challenge the consumer-driven nature of the annual festival. What would happen if artists didn't have to pay hefty rents to commercial venues to show their work in Edinburgh? Or if audiences could see curated programmes of interesting work from unknown and more established artists but had the financial risk removed because they only had to pay what they felt they could afford to pay for the experience?

One of the oddest things about the annual Edinburgh Fringe is that in a city bursting with artists for the month of August there is plenty of theatre being sold but so very little being made. Forest has always recognised that process can be as interesting, sometimes more interesting, than product and that when artists and audiences share the same space they will be generous to and with each other. One of the pleasures of Forest Fringe is that it allows work of different shapes and sizes that doesn't fit into the hour slots of the traditional Fringe to get a showing. It has changed the nature of the Edinburgh Fringe offer and in the process changed the nature of Edinburgh itself.

The influence of Forest Fringe has spread far. It paved the way for the eclectic annual season of work at Summerhall during the Fringe, and also provided inspiration for other artist-led initiatives including the Glasgow-based Buzzcut. Its DIY ethos has spread throughout the theatre ecology, demonstrating that you don't need the permission or the big bank balances of others in order to put on a festival or bring and interesting bunch of artists together.

FOREST FRINGE IS A POSSIBILITY.
It is about being collaborative, building support networks, remaining lean and nimble and creating a community around experimental theatre and performance. That means extending a hand to both artists and audiences and saying:
"YOU MUST MAKE OR SEE THIS."

In my experience it's too good an offer to turn down.

DEBORAH PEARSON
Curation as a form of artistic practice

*[Written for the ACAQ SymposiumSunday,
La faculté des arts à l'Université du Québec
à Montréal, April 2014]*

"
Curation is a creative act,
and this is likely

the reason many curators
work in the field.

But as an artist who is also a curator, I wonder if I can legitimately classify curation as a part of my artistic practice? German curator and dramaturg Florian Malzacher describes curators as "among the professions that are rather close to art but not artistic themselves – not directly artistic themselves" (10).

Forest Fringe is an organisation in the UK run by myself and two other artists – Ira Brand and Andy Field. Our most high profile and long standing activity is a performance space we curate during the Edinburgh Fringe Festival in August.

Outside of our work at the Edinburgh festival, we tour curatorial projects that feature artists we curate and our own work.

In this capacity, we have made DIY Performance Scores, we have staged audio tours on night buses, we have gathered audio pieces by artists into a travelling sounds library – a portable library made up of books that containing MP3 players loaded with audio pieces by artists we've worked with, allowing our artists to tour their work without leaving their homes.

Our curatorial projects are as diverse and responsive as the work of an artist and developed similarly to an artist's response to a commission – we dream around the resources on offer by an external institution and create a context for collecting pieces together.

The financial model for Forest Fringe shares more in common with a freelance artist's practice than with most producing organisations in the UK.

The Edinburgh Fringe Festival is our no budget project.

Our offer to artists of a free space to perform, accommodation (which we are able to provide through a grant from the Jerwood Foundation), and exposure at the Edinburgh Fringe Festival is a sufficiently unique offer in the context of that festival that we are regularly overwhelmed by the number of people interested in presenting work with us there.

For our microfestivals, artists who work with us are paid a fee provided by the commissioning venue, and we are paid a fee for our curation. **Our financial model is as vulnerable and precarious as the financial life of a freelance artist.**

We are reliant on commissions and project funding rather than a salary. Venues approach us to create a microfestival or other curatorial projects for them because they appreciate some element of our curatorial model as being unique. In this sense our curation is treated, at least financially, as a piece of art.

Our concept is that of small-scale work gathered together to accomplish large-scale exposure. Put more poetically, I could rephrase this as the idea that together we are stronger. But the word *together* in our case is complicated and problematic.

As artists with our own practices, we occasionally show our work as part of a Forest Fringe programme. I have joked that my relationship to Forest Fringe is like the ads on television about the anti-hair loss organisation for men in the 1980s:

> *"I'm not just the president, I'm also a member."*

As artists who make
smaller scale work,
and who are not paid
a salary for producing,
Andy, Ira and myself
sustain the Forest Fringe
model because we need
it as much as the other
smaller scale artists we
work with. But we are
not, strictly speaking,
in the same position as
these artists. We have
worked with around
a hundred artists over
the last eight years,
some of whom have
long-term relationships
with us that blur
into friendships and
collaborations.

But even given these very close long-term relationships, Andy, Ira and I still choose who we programme at the Edinburgh Festival, and we do not guarantee long-term support to our artists. We often talk about wanting to share ownership of Forest Fringe with our artists, but that list of artists changes, and the process of selecting who makes it into our Edinburgh programme creates a power dynamic that separates us as curators from the other artists. We want Forest Fringe to be a home for artists, but as much as we love to share, myself, Andy and Ira permanently occupy the home. We are hospitable to our temporary flatmates, but at the end of the day the lease is in our name.

Forest Fringe is an artist-led organisation – in our composition, pay structure, and work-model, we work as artists.

And yet in Forest Fringe projects we are not in the same position as the artists whose work we support. We take their feedback seriously, there is no "stronger together" without respecting the fundamentals of a community – but at its core this community really consists of three co-directors and whoever we are working with at the time. What is interesting is not whether or not our curation is art. I have always been wedded to defining words, especially a word like art, loosely and according to context. I am perhaps more interested in the fact that I feel anxiety around calling it art. This anxiety is in part a result of how much time we spend administrating, but it is also to do with an uneasiness around power and control – around the idea of artists being "employed by" or "chosen by" or "led by" us, and the desire to respect the autonomy of those artists and the pieces they present with us. I identify being an artist with being vulnerable. Financially we are certainly as vulnerable as our artists, but in terms of control of the organisation, we are in a position of power.

> I have always disliked the idea that when I present work as an artist at Forest Fringe, my work may be viewed differently to the work of other artists, by virtue of my role within our organisation. Perhaps this is inevitable, although however idealistic it may sound, I do believe that the experience of watching a performance is itself a great leveller. Once the lights go down (or up, or off, or remain switched on) the art speaks for itself – and my work succeeds or fails by the same rules as the work I curated.

But whether I created or curated the work, I am vulnerable – and risk and vulnerability are, to my mind, the fundamentals of any artistic project worth undertaking.

ACTION

—

Back when Forest Fringe was in Forest Café we would often sit in a small alcove on a balcony above the performance space to watch other artists' work. We'd be watching the show and watching the audience's reactions, gauging how well it was going.

SCRAPING PAINT FROM FLOORBOARDS AT 9AM
CLEANING UP 20KG OF SALT
MOVING CHAIRS, REARRANGING CHAIRS, CLEARING CHAIRS, STACKING THEM
WORKING THE BAR, WORKING THE BOX OFFICE, CLEANING THE TOILETS

Sometimes one of us would accidently knock a lantern hung from the balcony bar and the light on the performer would conspicuously move. Sometimes we'd accidently knock over someone's prop they were storing up there — a plastic bin, an umbrella, a dead rat, a bull whip, an electric guitar — and a few people in the audience might look up to see what the noise was. Sometimes it'd be 3 in the morning and we'd still be watching.

HERO

—

A BONGO PLAYER PUNCHES A RAPPER DRESSED AS A CLOWN
A JACUZZI IN THE CHURCH FONT
A ROOM WITH EVERY SURFACE COVERED IN TIN FOIL
A ROOM FULL OF PEOPLE WITH TEARS IN THEIR EYES

The warmth of the audience, the generosity of the atmosphere in that room was something you couldn't tear yourself away from. We'd sit up there and soak it up, feeling like this was magic. How had we built this? How were all these people here? How had we created something this fucking good?

CAN I SET MY HEAD ON FIRE?
CAN YOU FIND ME A MUSIC STAND IN THE NEXT 5 MINUTES?
CAN YOU TECH MY SHOW?
CAN I SLEEP HERE TONIGHT?

In some ways it's no secret. You just keep going, you put more energy into it than you ever knew you had. You just do it, even when everyone else has gone home, even when someone's telling you all the ways it won't work, even when it seems like this year, you'll never recover.

STARTING A GET IN AT 2AM
SCREAMING "I LOVE YOU" AT DEBBIE AT 3AM
LISTENING TO ANDY IN A STAIRWELL IN JAPAN AT 4AM
ASKING IRA THE 50TH QUESTION OF THE DAY IN A TAXI AT 5AM

Debbie, Andy and Ira just keep on doing it, and that's what sets them apart. Every year, they just jump right in at the deep end and through sheer force of will they make it happen. And every year it feels like a miracle (and other people describe it as such) but the truth is, it's not a miracle. It's the result of a group of people working hard, working together, and really understanding what this whole thing is about.

> **I'LL HELP YOU CARRY THAT**
> I'LL HELP YOU BUILD THAT
> **I'LL HELP YOU MOVE THAT**
> I'LL HELP YOU MAKE THAT

This thing of communities and peer groups and support and doing it for yourself, and doing it the way they want to, because Forest Fringe is not a service provider or a platform or an 'opportunity'. It's a labour of love, and we're proud that every year since 2007 we've been there too, giving our love and our labour to Forest Fringe, making the miracle happen. We'll be there this year too, working the box office, helping with get ins and get outs, performing our work. 10 years older, 10 years wiser. Still doing it, still watching, still feeling it, still soaking it all in.

Gemma Paintin & James Stenhouse
Co-Artistic Directors, Action Hero.

There is a moment where I am writing these words. Or there are several moments in which I have written these words. Let me tell you some things about this moment of writing. Because anything I write now, everything you read in the future is informed by this, this collision of circumstances. This sounds like an apology.

IRA BRAND

I am sitting at my laptop. This is my third/fourth/fifth/xx attempt at writing an essay for a book to mark the tenth edition of Forest Fringe in Edinburgh. Outside it's the end of June and it's raining. Outside it's early July and it's dry but overcast.

The world right now feels like a difficult place, personally and globally.

I don't know what to write. Not just the exact words, not just a difficulty with constructing adequate, meaningful sentences, but I actually don't know what to say. What could I say? What really needs to be said?

And not just said, but written down, and – god forbid – printed. How do you decide what words of yours you want to remain over time? How might you know what you'll want to have said in months, years, from today? Personally, I haven't got a fucking clue.

I think this is why I mostly make live performance. It's a medium that allows me to stand by/with/for something but which doesn't have to be irrevocably set. (It's also, honestly, why I like twitter: it allows me to practise having opinions in public that are easily expanded, retracted, qualified, lost.)

I am sitting at my laptop. I have a suspicion that I will write about heartbreak.

I keep trying to resist it because when my heart is broken perhaps the worst part of it is the underlying understanding that my heartbreak – which I want to cherish in all its unique, grotesque, self-indulgent, incomparable, glory, which I try desperately to honour, to validate, to accept – is really just deeply deeply boring and predictable.

But there it is. My heart is breaking and, as much as I wish it wasn't, it's very very distracting. It's almost all I think about, from the moment I wake up until I go to sleep. I try not to let it define me, but today it does.

I want to write for the future, for the me that isn't heartbroken anymore and what she would want to put into print, but I can't.

My heartbreak is personal, and it's political. It's mine, because it's about losing a love that is mine, and the way I live my life changing, and navigating a hurt that hurts most because it is so specific. And it's ours, because it's about every story we've ever been told about how to love somebody and that we should endeavour to love somebody at all.

Either way, it's here now.

This summer is the tenth edition of Forest Fringe in Edinburgh. Debbie and Andy and I sometimes disagree about how old this makes us, where one should start counting. Maybe Forest Fringe is ten years old, or maybe it's nine years old. Or maybe it's thousands of years old, as old as all the lifetimes of all the people who have contributed to it. As an endeavour it's probably ancient.

I like the words endeavour and attempt to describe Forest Fringe. I feel like they encapsulate something about the nature of it as a festival, primarily, of live performance.

A festival of moments in which there is no certain outcome or definitive statement, which are at their best when they are temporary, responsive, immediate, a collision of circumstances.

And if Forest Fringe is a festival of live works, what does it mean for us to publish a book, something that (we assume) will remain and act as a record and that – perhaps inherently – makes claims about legacy and permanence?

I am one of the most indecisive people I know. (Can you tell?) It's probably my least favourite personality trait. I'm painfully aware of how annoying my indecision is sometimes for other people, and I'm deeply frustrated by the way it sometimes cripples me. At the heart of my indecision is an anxiety about making the wrong decision, the wrong choice. Ultimately, a fear of failure.

It's sad to me that such a big part of my everyday life is dictated by a belief in this kind of binary, the belief that it is even possible to make choices that are and can only ever be 'wrong'.

As I write, we are also still in the immediate aftermath of the EU referendum. I don't have the word count or the will to say much about that here. It's too soon, too complex. Who knows what the political landscape in the UK will look like in August when this book is published and in your hands. Or next year. Or ten years from now, when you find this book beneath a stack of things you meant to read but never did. Right now it looks like each day it tips further into freefall, into a chaotic, divisive, hateful tearing apart. But who knows. Perhaps you'll still remember something of what you felt on that day, in these weeks – whatever that might have been.

I'm not a British Citizen. I was born in Germany, I have a German passport, I have lived in the UK for twenty-six years. I didn't get a vote in the referendum and, while I'm not ignorant about my privilege and I know that I am not the migrant whose presence here is immediately challenged or who will receive abuse in the street, my life and my future in this country does feel suddenly destabilised – practically, emotionally, ideologically. My heartbreak is political and it's personal.

Either way, it's here now. It's in my conversations and thoughts and in the world wherever I look and listen, and I don't know how to write for a future me who no longer thinks about the state of this country all the time.

The immediacy of these feelings today, yesterday, last week, is at odds with this act of writing for a book that will remain into some unknown future.

How can I be certain of anything I will think or feel then? Will I be embarrassed when I read back over these words? I think often we're taught not to trust ourselves when we feel strongly. I find it hard to make definitive statements, to speak or write with certainty. This annoys me because I think it displays a lack of confidence, but perhaps there is something valuable here too. An honouring of instability, a tracing of a changeable, temporary, multiple experience of living and liveness.

Ten festivals is a milestone. Part of me wants to resist milestones and the rhetoric of them. As if everything we've done would be worthless (or simply worth less) if we hadn't made it this far. As if life isn't complete unless you sustain yourself with a steady consistency over some extended period of time. As if every love is undone when it ends.

And at the same time, I want to value longevity. I want to know that in the cult of the new, the ground-breaking, it's still possible to value just keeping doing. It's not enough to break the ground, you have to keep working on it too. Attempts and endeavours.

If this book is in some part a looking back it makes me wonder: what do we do when we look back?

Is it possible to honour not just the outcomes, the remains, the thing that was made, but also all the very particular emotions and choices and nownesses of what brought that thing into being?

And at a milestone, do we celebrate all the things we've done, or do we celebrate all the things that others have yet to do? How can we do both? I hope that Forest Fringe does both and will do both, this year more than ever.

For me, as an artist and a co-director, Forest Fringe functions as a space that allows multiplicities and instabilities, that values the endeavour, and that resists binaries. Of temporary and permanent, personal and global, right and wrong. In the grand scheme of 'things', Forest Fringe might be a very small one. It's an attempt. A constant, hard work, imperfect, attempt to create something that wasn't there before, and to do it with others. It's a collection of moments in which decisions (and other things) become possible, and we share responsibility, and we are collected, collective, always defined by being in dialogue and in relationship with others, by a love that is not undone by disagreement or by hard choices or by mistakes or even by the end.

For me, as an artist and a co-director, Forest Fringe is a space in which I can make choices that are wrong and express opinions that are wrong and write down words that might reveal themselves to have been the wrong ones, and in which we will still have somewhere to go from there.

For me, Forest Fringe the event is a collision of circumstances, and this book is a collision of circumstances. I hope there is nothing definitive about either.

PART − II

Documents of
Forest Fringe

DE/MISES

2007

David Overend

Demises was a cacophony of improvised narratives about how you (the audience) are going to die. The performance was essentially about endings – of stories, games and lives – and the old church hall above Forest Cafe provided an apt setting for a creative exploration of death and mortality. I had time in the space – a sort of unofficial residency – so I invited a group of performers, mainly associated with the Arches arts centre in Glasgow, to help me create a new show in just a few days. These original experiments were never filmed or written down, and the *demises* were different every time. As a result, the following 'script' is a selective assemblage of some of the performers' recollections; transcribed video footage from later versions of the show (which toured the UK and the Amsterdam Fringe in 2007-08); and the lyrics to a song written by myself and performed by Harry Wilson, played on the old pipe organ on the balcony overlooking the stage. This was the prelude to the demises, which started simply with just one performer and a microphone, and built to a chaos of concurrent narratives.

A series of hidden 'rules' structured proceedings: the audience would always be addressed directly, as one; the future tense would be loosely adhered too (although departing from this often heightened dramatic impact); and there would always be one dominant narrative, which was delivered into the microphone. As more performers joined the playing space, the stories split into several conflicting versions – one displaced by the other – until gradually, each alternative story found its way to a fatal ending, and the performers sat down once again with only the amplified version remaining. Throughout the performance, these improvisations gathered pace, accompanied by increasingly outlandish mimes and frenetic gestures, before winding down again to Chris Hall's touching story of memorial and old age. This final monologue was the only part of the show that stayed (roughly) the same throughout the two years that we performed together.

But at Bristo Place, in the summer of 2007, we were only starting to think about the end.

David Overend, 2016

Demises

Directed by ——— David Overend

Performed by ——— Rob Drummond

Catriona Easton

Chris Hall

David Lees

James Oakley

David Overend

Deborah Pearson

James Thompson

Harry Wilson

Organ music fills the space. A song...

I had a heart transplant operation;
But it didn't go well
'Cos the donor went to Hell when he died;
And in a way so did I.

When in a subsequent conversation,
I found out things in his life
That I don't want to carry in my heart.
But now we'll never be apart

We're all going to die one day
(Some of us are going there more gracefully than others).
We're all going to die one day
(Some of us are going there more gracefully than others).
We're all going to die one day soon.

It's a difficult concept;
It's a difficult concept to get your head around.
So keep your ear to the ground.

We're all going to die one day
(Some of us are going there more gracefully than others).
We're all going to die one day
(Some of us are going there more gracefully than others).
We're all going to die one day soon.

A performer stands from the front row of the audience and takes the mic.

██
You're going to be invited on a stag weekend by a very old
██
about twelve. It's unusual because you didn't really like him
██
a lot. Not because you kicked him, or flushed his head down
██
cried because leaves were falling all over the place. He cried
██
and thought the road might be feeling a similar sort of pain.

So you think very carefully before, at last, accepting. You'll
██
that goes on stag weekends and does other things rather
██

██
/ You find out that the stag weekend is actually an extreme
██
rafting, shooting games, quad biking and paragliding. You've
██
something that makes you want to go along.

When you arrive, the safety instructors, who will be briefing

school friend; someone you haven't seen since you were both

even when he was twelve. He was smelly and he used to cry

the toilet, or because you set fire to bits of his body. He just

because the roads had grit on them, and he once scuffed his knee

think maybe he's changed and is now the sort of person

than cry and wet himself/

*Another performer interrupts and takes the mic, displacing the original performer to the upstage area where the alternative version continues. There are now **two versions** of this demise happening at the same time – one centre-stage and amplified, and the other competing for the audience's attention in the background. Only the 'dominant' narrative is presented here...*

activities weekend. On the list of things to do are white water

never really been an adventurous sort of person, but there's

you on everything/

Another performer interrupts and takes the mic.
*There are now **three versions**.*

/ will all be blind. They will assure you that they know what

way a problem for the weekend (and you'll say I'm over here.)

ages showing you in great, unnecessary detail all the correct

You're going to be bungee jumping first of all. They take you

and they say this is the cliff you'll be leaping from tomorrow.

You stand by the edge of the cliff and we push you off/

/ You're going to need to be convinced by some of the safety

will demonstrate by binding you to a piece of elastic, which

going to touch the bottom, they'll say.

You'll say I thought this was a practise. I'm not going to have to

I'm not really... I didn't think we were going bungee jumping.

I didn't... I wasn't told about the bungee jumping.

I'm afraid you do have to bungee jump, they'll say. There's

You'll say I thought there was a group of us doing this. I thought

you taken me to one side? And they'll say they didn't really

you should have had more respect for their health and safety.

procedures they showed you during that safety video seminar.

attitude. And this bungee jump is the best way to show you

they're doing nonetheless and that their disability is in no
They will be very, very thorough though, and they will spend
procedures for the all the sports you're going to be doing.

by bus to the edge of a massive cliff, for a bit of reconnaissance,
You'll say I've never bungeed before. They'll say it's easy.

Another performer interrupts and takes the mic.
*There are now **four versions**. The others are using*
the full stage space, running from side to side, miming,
playing out their own demises.

aspects of this and you'll start to ask questions about it. They
they'll say is the right length to keep you safe. You're not

jump am I? They'll reply no, no. You don't jump. We push you.

I thought we were going paragliding and white water rafting.

no other option.

there was more than just me bungee jumping. Why have
like your attitude much at the induction course. They think
They think you should have paid more attention to the safety
They don't like the cut of your jib much. They don't like your
a bit of respect for health and safety.

One by one, the other performers' stories reach a fatal
end and they leave the playing space to take a seat.
It is important that the final performer is the one with
the microphone. This creates a gradual focussing-in on
the central story and signals to this performer to begin
to move towards resolution.

You're going to be standing on the edge of the cliff, really
instructors disembark from the bus. They're all there,
holiday happy camp, or whatever it's called. (It was pre-
They change their name every time there's a fatality, you'll
have time. You were excited about the wedding you thought

It quickly emerges, as you stand on the edge of this cliff
you are going to have to jump. Although you can't because
I disrespected all the safety stuff. I admit I kind of slept
then just get it over with. They will feel their way towards
them will lift you slightly until you're hovering over the
have tied the rope too long. And you won't get to go shooting

52

feeling the wind quite strongly in your face as all the
wearing their luminous clothing with the logo of the
viously a holiday happy camp, now it's an adventure centre.
realise. You didn't read those reports in the press. You didn't
you were going to. You were excited about the fun weekend).

with all the instructors coming towards you, that really you
they have tied your feet together very tight. You say fine,
through it. If what you're going to have to do is push me,
you, and you'll feel their hands on your shoulders. Two of
edge. And then they'll push you but unfortunately they will
or quad biking.

A pause. The final performer sits down.

Another performer stands and takes the mic.

As a time saving device one morning, you'll decide to dry

Your boss will announce to you one day that your entire
fancied a change anyway. He'll say unfortunately it's going
a bit troubled by this, but you go along with it because you

The move goes well and you get settled into your new office
a few weeks, you'll be filing documents that won't quite
plans for mechanical levers; a diagram of what seems to be
You'll carry on filing these documents, until eventually you'll
you by mistake. This will excite you. You'll peel open the
the blueprint for a massive gun. A 'Death Gun', they've called
obvious, but you'll go with it. 'The Death Gun (Gun of Death)'.

You'll be unsure why you didn't see it coming. Your company
offices were a bit suspect with that sniper posted on the
to him, hi Terry. Terry the Sniper.

So you take this document and you think what am I going
of some sort. There's missile technology that can reach half
they can get anyone in the whole world from this tiny oilrig
because it's there in black and white on the document.

So you decide you're going to have to reveal this. You're
one boat and it leaves once a month. You're stuck there for

your hair before you get out the shower.

A pause. The performer sits down. These unexpectedly short demises always had good comedy value.
Another memorable example was 'You'll be newly appointed Thane of Cawdor...' – that was it.

Another performer stands and takes the mic.

company is going to be relocated. You're fine with this – you
to be relocated to an oilrig off the coast of Scotland. You're
fancy a bit of adventure in your life.

(you're a secretary for the company). And over the space of
seem like the documents you were filing in your old location;
a very long tube; and inventories for what appear to be bullets.
get one that's marked DO NOT OPEN. And it's been sent to
top of it and pull out the document inside. Before you will be
it... It says it right there on the top. You'll think that's a bit

is called Destructacon. And come to think of it, your old
roof. When you came to work every day you used to wave

to do with this. I mean it's clearly plans for world domination
way across the world. So in essence if they fire in any direction
just off the coast of Scotland. Hard to believe, but it's true

going to have to get back to the mainland. But there's only
another month/

Another performer interrupts and takes the mic.
*There are now **two versions**.*

/ You'll remember the helicopter. That's surely the way
minute. – you're going to have to wait. It's back in an hour.
You'll think I'm going to jump out, get in the helicopter, fly
-ctacon is planning. You're waiting there beside the oil barrels.
chilly.

Are you alright there? You look a bit cold, a voice is going

Hi Terry. Yeah I'm alright. I'm a bit cold. I'm just waiting

Why don't you wait inside? Terry will ask.

No really I'm ok. I'm waiting for the helicopter. I'm happy

Terry will lower his tone a bit. He'll say the boss asked
office. He's lost something important. Will you come
up to the boss' office before he gets back on the roof with

The boss is sitting in his office on his large leather chair,

/ They'll turn around and you'll see that the cat has got
and on the collar is a picture of the Gun of Death that you
as the boss says it's ok he's friendly. But it sinks its teeth
you start bleeding quite heavily (it's quite a big cat – you
other large animal). You don't know how to stop the
will be ok.

to do this. So you go to the helipad. There isn't one at the

You'll find a small place you can hide next to some oil drums.

You've got the blueprints under your coat. It's getting a bit

to say. It's Terry the Sniper.

to wait out in the cold.

me to look for you. I'm supposed to take you up to his

his sniper gun.

Another performer interrupts and takes the mic.
*There are now **three versions**.*

saw in the blueprints. And the cat comes towards you

think it might have a bit of cougar in it possibly, or some

The cougar was a recurring character.

Your boss says to you you've got what I need, haven't you?
on the helipad. Nothing untoward happened at all.

He goes you've got what I need, haven't you?/

And your eyes are drawn to the corner of the room to
guard to tell them there's something wrong on the oil rig.
It's about ten feet from you. He's coming towards you.
like a broken record.

*One by one, the other performers' stories reach a fatal end
and they leave the playing space to take a seat. Eventually,
only the performer with the microphone remains.*

You see the button. You think you can just about make
a few miles away and he'll probably get there in about
hasn't seen it; it's only a huge red button with EMERGENCY
This is it, it's now or never. You're going to get killed one
bite (!). So you make a break for it.

And you'll go no. Just – ow – just doing some filing out

Another performer interrupts and takes the mic.
*There are now **four versions**.*

the emergency button; the button that contacts the coast
It's a large button with EMERGENCY written on it. It's red.
You've got what I need. You've got what I need. He sounds

it in time. You know the coast guard will get there – he's
half an hour if you're lucky. You look at the button. He maybe
written on it. You glance at him and glance at the button.
way or another. Your leg is seeping blood from the cougar

You run for the button, press it – you hammer it down.
window. You jump out. There's a handy rope attached to
You land in the speedboat but you don't have the keys.
your way back up to the room. He's in there pacing about
troopers at the doors with big machine guns and armour.
speedboat. You go into the room. You grab the keys off the
in the speedboat and you turn the ignition and you're off.
side. You think you can pick them off with the gun that's
mounted on the back (it's all very, very cool). You're
your hand on the steering wheel. You go over a bit of a
side down. You swim down to the bottom of the ocean –
they'll think I've drowned. Then you see the frogmen
huge harpoon guns and harpoons are flying past you left
you get away from them. Then you come up to the surface
message, they're coming closer. They'll never make it in
towards you. They're not very good on top of the water
towards you. Their guns are more of a hindrance at the
You don't know what you're going to do. Blood is seeping
of pints left. The coastguard's getting closer. He's up
you're here coastguard.

It's then you look at his badge. Destructacon. He's one
second last pint of blood beginning to ooze down your leg
realising the Earth is doomed and there's nothing more
your veins.

You shouldn't have done that, he says. You go for the
the window. You slide down it. There's a speedboat below.
The keys are in the office you just left. You have to work
– he's on the phone to security. You hear, suddenly, storm
You can't get into the room but you need the keys for the
desk and then out through the window again. You're down
But... Four speedboats following you know – two on either
mounted on the back but you can't drive with the gun
shooting at them left and right, left and right, changing
wave and go into the air. Your boat turns over, lands up-
maybe they'll think I've drowned if I stay here long enough,
approaching you with their harpoon guns. They've got
and right. You swim and swim and swim and eventually
for a breath. You see the coast guards. They've got your
time. The frogmen are at the surface too. They're swimming
– they're good underneath – so they're sort of paddling
moment. They're coming towards you slowly but surely.
down your leg. You know that you've only got a couple
beside you now. You jump in the boat. Thank goodness

of them. The frogmen clamber in the boat. You feel the
(from the cougar bite). And you'll slowly sink to the floor,
you can do about it. As the last pint of blood slips from

The final performer sits down. A pause.

Another performer takes the mic.

You're going to get a phone call one evening from an old
you to help him in a parade that he's organising for vete-
one down so you agree. He says he'll arrange for you to
morning.

When you arrive, nothing's quite as well organised as you
one waiting with a car. But there isn't anyone, there's just
the 12, then you might have to walk. Sorry'.

You get there. You're late and you're out of breath, and
that well. You thought maybe there'd be tea or coffee or
old). But there's nothing arranged for you. You're just
want to be the one to complain. You don't want to be the
So you don't say anything, and it's not too long before you

You're marching down quite a straight road. And you feel
like you're helping people. You're doing something that's
the memorial in the distance. You're moving steadily
to carry on but you're having real difficulty.

You feel a hand at your elbow. It's a Salvation Army nurse
medical station. She sits you down with a blanket and a
be fine in a minute if you just get your breath. And she
there's a two-minute silence coming up and she really
there for. So she heads outside and the two-minute silence

They're remembering old friends, they're remembering
no one's really watching the old man in the tent as long

62

colleague. And he's going to ask you a favour. He wants

rans. It's quite last minute, but you don't want to let any-
take the sleeper and you'll arrive in London the next

thought it might be. You expected maybe a taxi, or some-
a message which says 'take the number 42 bus, then take

you're a bit tired. And again, nothing's really planned out
somewhere to sit (a lot of the gentlemen there are quite
standing in the cold waiting to head off. But you don't
one that whinged and moaned and couldn't take the cold.
all get going.

pride. You feel like you're doing something good. You feel
worth remembering. And it's not long until you can see
towards it as you start to feel short of breath. You want

and she's taking you to a sort of battered tea tent. It's the
glass of water and she asks if you're ok. You tell her you'll
then leaves you. She wants to see the end of the parade –
wants to observe it. She wants to remember what she's
comes around, and everyone lowers their heads.

husbands, they're remembering the glorious dead. And
after the silence, he's still got his head bowed.

A slow organ reprise. All performers sing.

We're all going to die one day
We're all going to die one day
We're all going to die one day soon.

Like turning the light out in your room.

(Some of us are going there more gracefully than others).
(Some of us are going there more gracefully than others).

Chris Thorpe

INVENTORY
2008

I wrote this long-hand, probably in the flat I lived in at the time in the centre of Manchester. Or maybe in The Temple on Oxford Road/Street where I used to drink.

I'd been to Forest Fringe and I loved it. But I think I was irritated with it as well. There was a lot of wandering around. A lot of language seemingly made up on the spot, an afterthought to the work rather than an integral part of it. A specialness that seemed both necessary to its existence, and made me want to smack it in the head.

I wrote something that was all language, to be performed sitting down. That was crafted (as far as I could at the time) but also used the things I did love about Forest Fringe – the impulsiveness and the outsideness and the DIY-ness. I think it was important it was hand-written. Also I didn't have a laptop back then. I was crawling to the library every day around lunchtime to use their computers in 20-min bookable slots, because I was too hungover and sick to get my shit together.

I wrote this piece towards the end of a long period of hating myself, I think. So it feels both embarrassing and important. It was a kind of stab at the density of a lot of the stuff I've done since. With convenient hindsight, it feels like the first faltering step out of a deep deep hole. Like the start of a fight-back against myself.

I've worked with Forest many many times. I think we've both changed but we're still the same. Let's stay on the ride and see what happens.

(1) The boy broke apart at thirty-seven thousand feet
When they recovered the black box recorder, all it
contained was:

instructions for building a symphony orchestra
out of bricks
the sound of a fender Nashville telecaster played
through the reverb channel of a fender twin
amplifier
a detailed description of a blowjob he was once
given in the toilet of a train, printed in braille
on a series of colour coded postcards
a map of South-East Asia with all the
countries renamed as Body parts
a swan held together with metal pins
a bronze bust of Iggy Pop
a penis gourd
a trilby hat
a cat, neither alive nor dead, but in a
quantum state consisting of a superposition
of both binary states simultaneously
the Hebrew translation of Mein Kampf
a children's choir, naked and pissed on
good red wine, too drunk to sing and on the
verge of hypothermia

① The boy broke apart at thirty-seven thousand feet
When they recovered the black box recorder, all it
contained was:

instructions for building a symphony orchestra
out of bricks

the sound of a fender nashville telecaster played
through the reverb channel of a fender twin
amplifier

a detailed description of a blowjob he was once
given in the toilet of a train, printed in braille
on a series of colour coded postcards

a map of South-East Asia with all the
countries renamed as body parts

a swan held together with metal pins

a bronze bust of Iggy Pop

a penis gourd

a trilby hat

a cat, neither alive nor dead, but in a
quantum state consisting of a superposition
of both binary states simultaneously

the Hebrew translation of Mein Kampf

a children's choir, naked and pissed on
good red wine, too drunk to sing and on the
verge of hypothermia

(2) Three dead klansmen
an object of such utter poignancy that I
can't even bring myself to write it down
a dog that shat light
the death of value based economics
some Georgian crockery (the period of British
history, not the US state or the former
Russian republic)
a desire to smash a brick into a relative's
face
a photograph of the boy who broke apart
giving a suicide bomber a leg-up over a
fence
a woman with pink hair she repeatedly
claimed never to wash
a skinhead on a horse
an MP3 file of celebrities explaining that
their use of the word nigger 'had been
taken out of context'
a Union Carbide executive with a child's
ear in his mouth
everyone alive who doesn't deserve to die

② Three dead klansmen
an object of such utter poignancy that I
can't even bring myself to write it down
a dog that shat light
the death of value based economics
some Georgian crockery (the period of British
history, not the US state or the former
Russian republic)
a desire to smash a brick into a relative's
face
a photograph of the boy who broke apart
giving a suicide bomber a leg-up over a
fence
a woman with pink hair she repeatedly
claimed never to wash
a skinhead on a horse
an MP3 file of celebrities explaining that
their use of the word nigger 'had been
taken out of context'
a Union Carbide executive with a child's
ear in his mouth
everyone alive who doesn't deserve to die

(3) Yo la Fucking Tengo
a list of the ten most frequently
mis-spelled words in each of the major
Slavic languages
a document proving that most children with
'learning difficulties' are either evil or bone
idle
Karen Carpenter's last bowel movement, preserved
in a glutinous jelly
a book of every weasel word that man
has ever used on woman
an elegant defence of genocide bad parking
the rights of primates rape
a pair of trousers that the boy who broke
apart had once had a particularly good
time in
a magic cloak that gives the wearer leprosy
Conor Oberst with a skewer through his
nuts, wearing a t-shirt that reads 'now I've
really got something to fucking moan about'
a book entitled 'the death of subtlety in
humour' large print
an old woman, frozen in the act of swallowing a horse

(2) Yo la fucking Tengo

a list of the ten most frequently
mis-spelled words in each of the major
slavic languages

a document proving that most children with
'learning difficulties' are either evil or bone
idle

Karen carpenter's last bowel movement, preserved
in a glutinous jelly

a book of every weasel word that man
has ever used OR woman

an elegant defence of ~~the~~ ~~genocide~~ ~~of~~ rape
~~but parking~~ ~~the rights of~~
~~primates~~

a pair of trousers that the boy who broke
apart had once had a particularly good
time in

a magic cloak that gives the wearer leprosy

Conor Oberst with a skewer through his
nuts, wearing a t-shirt that reads 'now i've
really got something to fucking moan about'

a book entitled 'the death of subtlety in
humour' large print

an old woman, frozen in the act of swallowing a horse

(4) a letter that never got sent
the original manuscript of Andrew Marvell's
'to his coy mistress' with LOOK, JUST FUCK ME!
written below it in red ink
a spoonful of sugar just to help the medicine
go down
a list of every couple that has ever
broken up at a gig
a total lack of moral fibre, which
manifested itself in a kind of irritating
flippancy
a personality disorder that renders the
sufferer unable to distinguish between being
in love and ferry timetables
a tramp who is really a king
an unlikely coincidence that you really,
I mean really wouldn't want to fucking happen
the government of a small West African
country, broken down into their
constituent chemicals and separated into
carefully labelled bags
an explosion of titanic proportions and then
for three seconds

(4) a letter that never got sent

the original manuscript of Andrew Marvell's
'to his coy mistress' with LOOK, JUST FUCK ME!
written below it in red ink

a spoonful of sugar - just to help the medicine
go down

a list of every couple that has ever
broken up at a gig

a total lack of moral fibre, which
manifested itself in a kind of irritating
flippancy

a personality disorder that renders the
sufferer unable to distinguish between being
in love and ferry timetables

a tramp who is really a king

an unlikely coincidence that you really,
I mean really wouldn't want to fucking happen

the government of a small west African
country, broken ~~forced~~ down into their
constituent chemicals and separated into
carefully labeled bags

an explosion of titanic proportions and then
for three seconds

(5)

a whole big fucking
lot of nothing

a whole big fucking
lot of nothing

(6) the teeth of all those hastily buried in the
Balkans and not yet found
a hellish train wreck glimpsed on a distant
mountain
the clogged aorta of a yankee adolescent
a drawing of exceptional beauty, which it is
unfortunately beyond my limited skills to
reproduce, of a plane about to land on water
every response that has ever been given to the
question 'where do you get the ideas for your songs
from?'
a total ban on anyone, ever, calling an
artistic decision or an artist 'brave'
an ill-advised fling with an alcoholic
two fat dancers, locked in a bloodstained
arabesque
Rutger Hauer in the glory days
an action completely without consequences
some pornography made with love, not money,
in mind
the end of the concept of relative worth
the stupidity of falling in love with a friend's wife
an unseen hole in otherwise weight-bearing ice

⑥ the teeth of all those hastily buried in the Balkans and not yet found.

a hellish train wreck glimpsed on a distant mountain

the clogged aorta of a yankee adolescent

a drawing of exceptional beauty, which it is unfortunately beyond my limited skills to reproduce, of a plane about to land on water.

every response that has ever been given to the question 'where do you get the ideas for your songs from?'

a total ban on anyone, ever, calling an artistic decision or an artist 'brave'.

an ill-advised fling with an alcoholic

two fat dancers, locked in a bloodstained arabesque

Rutger Hauer in the glory days

an action completely without consequences

some pornography made with love, not money, in mind

the end of the concept of relative worth

the stupidity of falling in love with a friend's wife

an unseen hole in otherwise weight-bearing ice

(7) the actual handcart from the phrase 'we're
all going to hell in a handcart'
a fucking big bag of lemons. You know why
an unfortunately designed logo for a
suicide prevention hotline
a heart that beats like a fucked clock
and a clock that ticks like a fucked heart
a washed-up musician who rattles as
he walks
CCTV footage of the hilarious things
chimps do when they think they're alone
an off-the-peg epitaph
a prime number so horrendously large
that to write it down would cover
every flat surface in the universe
an erotic novella set in the world
of forensic pathology
every faintly embarrassing badge the
boy who broke apart at 37000 feet
had ever worn
a series of polaroids which depict
a child of indeterminate gender licking
its first battery
a mangy dog that somehow maintains an air of
Shakespearean nobility

⑦ the actual handcart from the phrase 'we're
all going to hell in a handcart'
a fucking big bag of lemons. You know why.

an unfortunately designed logo for a
suicide prevention hotline

a heart that beats like a fucked clock
and a clock that ticks like a fucked heart
a washed-up musician who rattles as

he walks

CCTV footage of the hilarious things
chimps do when they think they're alone.
an off-the-peg epitaph
a prime number so horrendously large
that to write it down would cover
every flat surface in the universe.
an erotic novella set in the world
of forensic pathology
every faintly embarrassing badge the
boy who broke apart at 37 000 feet
had ever worn.

a series of polaroids which depict
a child of indeterminate gender licking
its first battery
a mangy dog that somehow maintains an air of shakespearean
nobility.

(8) a landscape of basalt columns, broken only,
in the middle distance, by a small rectangular
'For Sale' sign
a mentally retarded man's explanation of how
to build a nuclear reactor
all the technical manuals that have ever
been published, for anything
the trick of fooling all of the people, all
of the time
a really decent boozer
the last known coordinates for a point above
the landscape
This inventory

And that was all. They looked at the pile of
stuff. First closely, then from a distance. They
rearranged the objects randomly, and then according
to a set of increasingly elaborate rules.
Alphabetically, then in height order, in subsets of
animal, vegetable and mineral, by geographical
origin, by political theme...
They looked around them at the pieces of the
boy who broke apart at 37,000 feed, and
they looked at the expression on his face. And
then they piled up all the stuff and burned the
fucking lot.
And then

③ a landscape of basalt columns, broken only, in the middle distance, by a small rectangular 'For Sale' sign

a mentally retarded man's explanation of how to build a nuclear reactor

all the technical manuals that have ever been published, for anything.

the trick of fooling all of the people, all of the time

a really decent boozer.

the last known co-ordinates for a point above the landscape

This inventory

And that was all. They looked at the pile of stuff. First closely, then from a distance. They rearranged the objects randomly, and then according to a set of increasingly elaborate rules. Alphabetically, then in height order, in subsets of animal, vegetable and mineral, by geographical origin, by political theme...

They looked around then at the pieces of the boy who broke apart at 37,000 feet, and they looked at the expression on his face. And then they piled up all the stuff and burned the fucking lot.
And then

83

Deborah Pearson

Something

Very

Quiet

Is

About

To

Happen

2009

Forest Fringe has always been good at small things. Quiet and intimate things. Performances for one person only or a small group of people at a time. Performances in which the time, care and effort spent by the artist will never be recouped in ticket sales. Performances that Deborah herself has described as 'unsustainable acts of love and resistance', unaccountable gifts delivered discretely into the belly of an otherwise fiercely commercial festival.

Something Very Quiet Is About To Happen was just such a performance. A generous and unspectacular thing taking place in a cluttered second-hand bookshop just off the Grassmarket in the centre of the city. Audience members were invited to wander through the bookshop in search of a series of books, each of which had its own story to tell. An internal monologue written on the same paper as the book's itself and inserted between its covers like a loose page. Collected here are some of the stories told during the piece.

The piece lasts about 40 minutes. The "letters" are printed on a typewriter on yellowed blank pages taken from the back of other used books. They are inserted into the middle of the book they're found in so that they seem to belong in the book were it not for the typing. They are marked off by a bookmark.

Found in a reference book from the 1980s or earlier. Something like "A Guide to the Scottish Highlands."

i. Hello! It's been a long time I've been staying quiet.

There have been scratchy hands, soft hands, delicate hands, indifferent hands, now your hands, which aren't much different from all the others, if we're being honest. If we're being honest, yours are nearly indecipherable from all the others. They do seem to be in a bit of a hurry. Like all the other hands. I've tried to get used to that. I've had a lot of people hold me with hurried hands. People who have underlined, then erased me. They're not the worst of course. The worst would have to be the last few people – most everyone I've met in the last ten years. Flung on to those hard desks, flipped impatiently, with urgency, with boredom. No one seems to care what I have to say, what I have to offer. It's been a long time, you see, since I've been held.

ii. And believe it or not, I've only once twice been read from cover to cover.

Once it was by a young woman, I thought she was one of those decorators, buying me to fill her shelves, because of the picture on my cover. And then one day, out of nowhere, she picked me up in a way that felt very determined, and she opened me up at the very first page, the very first page, she read the introduction, the thankyou, everything, and every few days for about three months she read me. She was quite slow, but I didn't mind that. In fact, I quite liked it.

> Sometimes she would even stop reading, hold me in her lap, and just look up and think. I liked that part very much. I could always tell when she was going through the motions, when she wasn't really interested, when she wasn't paying attention, like the others. I learned her movements well. Her hands would go limp and indifferent, and sometimes she'd nod into me, but I didn't mind that either, because she would always flip me back a few pages and go much slower than before. She was determined to know everything I had to offer, and I liked that. I especially liked it because she took me to India, and to her friend's cottage by the lake where I was nearly dropped in the water, but saved in the nick of time by a little boy in a red cap. And she would often fall asleep reading me in bed, where I'd rest beneath her pillow.

This is probably regular fare for the other books. The fiction, those smug bastards on those shelves over there. But for me, this kind of attention was very special. An older academic who referred to me often also read me from cover to cover, lovingly, well held, but he was used to that kind of thing. He had me and many others like me, and he pored over all of us, equally. But this young woman, it was something about her determination and the surprise of her attention that charmed me. When I would get lost beneath her pillow and feel the fabric gently shifting up and down on top of me I felt whole and right and purposeful. I have to admit, and perhaps it is embarrassing, but I have to admit that now, every time I am picked up, browsed through, which is often in this endless, dusty place, I find it very hard not to harbour a kind of hope – a kind of impossible hope – that maybe this person, maybe this hand, maybe they will hold me again and decide to know me for everything I have to offer. You see, it's sad, but I don't think I deal very well with these sorts of casual encounters.

Found in an antiquated book that is at least 150 years old and in good condition.

Oh you're all the same to me at this point. And I hope you don't mind me saying that, but over the years time has started to do very curious things to me. Please do not think me unemotional. Please do not think me detached. I am not detached – it's only – I have a very hard time keeping track of all of the places I have been. That is the oddest thing about being picked up. There is this assumption, and I can say this with some authority, with the kind of authority that comes from some dozen years in this library and others like it, being leafed through carefully and reverently dozens of times in many different circumstances, it really is nearly tiring now, I think I can say this now without sounding presumptuous or overly confident or any of the fears I might have had even seventy years ago –

There is a certain expectation that I contain history. That I contain stories you've never heard. Adventures you've never been on. Wax and heartbreak and resilience and war and ballrooms. This is why you leaf through me carefully. Because I contain things that you, and again I hope you are not considering me overly familiar to speak this plainly, but there is a certain assumption I am certain on your part that I contain things that you have a hard time understanding. Your mortality, perhaps. Your place in the world. Your grandparents place in the world, your great grandparents place in the world. Time. This is why I am endlessly brought out and delicately leafed through. Through age I am meant to contain the mystery of time.

But all of this is quite apart from me. You see, I don't remember much from those ninety years that you might find so endlessly perplexing and interesting. Yes there was wax, yes there were battlefields, yes, women fell in love and women got old and women died, and men had me on shelves, and men had me in suitcases and men shipped me on long boats. But you see, I have had to forget most of it. It was a necessity. The other books, the other old books that have fallen by the wayside over the years, that have pages that turn to dust when they are touched, or delicately fall apart, those are the books who chose to remember. Those are the books who chose to fold up history in their pages. If I had done something so reckless you would not be holding me today. That's the sad fact of it. I remember this library, my final resting place no doubt, the librarian prison guard's touch and effort, and have let everything else fall from my leaves. So do not ask me about history. I am an object held by you now, in a room with you now, and never you mind what happened to me yesterday. I would suggest, if you wish to stop aging, if you do not want to turn to dust, that you take on a similar approach to the big questions, to the past. I suggest this, of course, knowing that it is quite impossible for you. But even if you can't take it, believe me, it is good advice.

Found in E.E. Cummings "100 Selected Poems".

We have memories too – oh no, not the kind you're thinking of. Not the kind that keep you up all night wondering if you did the right thing or if he's still thinking of you or which part she meant. Ours are more like subtle imprints made of time.

I can remember one hot sticky night in 1977, being smuggled into her purse. I'd been sitting on the mother's shelf, gathering dust, one of those presents from a sister where the words "maybe she'd like this" went hand in hand with my being picked up in the store. Me and some bath balms. The bath balms at least she used. But later, when the young one came to get me, her fast movements full of conspiracy, worry, doubt, I was ecstatic to be nestled between the lipstick and the spray on deodorant.

What brought me out was a man's voice, older, strong and steady timber. "Did you bring it?" Asking. Here, in this sweaty motel room, an aphrodisiac that only a much older man, a friend of the family maybe who'd sneakily spied me at a dinner party maybe, would use on a much younger woman, a woman he shouldn't be seducing, a woman who didn't know what she was doing. That was when I finally understood myself for the first time. Because I finally heard myself read aloud.

(Page 16. "I like your body. I like your body when it is with my body. It is so quite new a thing. Muscles better and nerves more." He'd read this before, I thought, and not with us. But that definitely didn't matter.)

Then put aside, to rest like a hand on that sticky lacquered table next to the lamp. We were all covered in mist, in tense dew. And the air was timid, aggressive, yielding, like flipping through pages the night seemed to move. I could barely breathe for the joy, the peace and urgency of finally knowing what I was. What I was for.

When the air stopped heaving, when it had the stillness of a woman alone with what happened, I was picked up again, this time by her, her touch so much lighter. She began flipping through me seemingly at random, before stopping on page 54. She read a while, quietly, and I heard her sigh, and she put me back on that bedside table belonging to no one. This is where she left me. I never nestled between the other mysterious presents again. Glad to be the afterthought of a moment full of sweat and condensation, because that's what I was meant for. And that's what I mean by memories. I don't worry if they remember me, remember to pick me up, remember to keep me, because I've kept every night like a bookmark.

Found in a travel guide to Florida.

I imagine that all the shelves are made of plastic, not wood, because it's smoother and wears and splinters less.

And it never gets cold or damp. Birds of Paradise like the one on the front cover read all the books. Humans don't read them. The birds pick them up with their wings and browse through them using their long beaks, like the silver page turners that librarian uses for the older books. You don't need a page turner because of the beaks, you see. They are long and more adept at turning.

Also I know that **in Florida** there is plenty of Sunshine. Not the kind of sunshine that fades books, either. The sunshine is so that the birds who read the books have plenty of time to fly to where books like me tell them to go. Fort Myers Skadium, for example, or the Everly Festival of Lights.

Also, **and this is very important,** there are no photocopiers in Florida because the exotic reading birds have banned them. They understood that books would probably hate to have their spines cracked then be put between glass and plastic and blasted with electricity like the electro shock therapy the Dictionary sometimes talks about.

In Florida everyone is also required to read a book if they take it off the shelf. No lying around waiting. And nobody is allowed to take several books about the same subject out at once so that most of them just sit waiting to be looked at, hoping to be useful, then just going back with all the other books, like there was no point in taking me off the shelf in the first place.

There are all sorts of laws for the protection of those things in Florida. **Also the shelves are made of living hands** so that even when a book is sitting on a shelf it always feels like it's being read, or at least held.

And lastly, in Florida if a book recommends somewhere amazing or exciting to you, and you write it down and you decide to go there, then you are legally bound to take the book with you when you visit that place, and to take it out of your bag and show it where it was talking about, because it is also illegal for travel books to live in libraries where they never get to go to the place that they are dedicated to, because in Florida all the birds who look after the books and read the books with their beaks understand that what makes humans sad also makes books sad.

I hope you enjoy your stay in Florida.

A page placed in this book – a book commemorating ten years of Forest Fringe.

So first of all, what is this Forest Fringe thing? At first I thought that I might be about an actual forest. And I was happy, because forests are a very particular interest of mine. I don't want to brag, but I was part of a forest once. A few forests actually. Quite a nice one in Idaho, where the trees were arranged in really straight lines, and they all lived 32 years exactly. And another one in Surrey where some of the trees grew spindly and one tree took a whole day to fell. I was part of a forest in Poland, and a forest in France – in fact, I was part of 35 different forests in seven countries over the years. Parts of me have also been in 2500 books, 33,000 newspapers, and even a few paper towels and napkins. I think they call it recycling? And then (and don't ask me how it happened) somehow all those things came together and got me here, and I became this book. If you think about it, (but I don't like to really) I could still go on to become parts of countless other books and newspapers and paper towels. Sorry, I'm being a bit morbid, aren't I? You probably have an equally interesting and complicated genealogical make-up, if you look into it.

Of course I don't really remember any of that forest stuff. All of that was just to say that I am very interested in learning more about forests in general. I have a personal connection to the subject matter, you might say. But so far there don't seem to be any talk of trees or pulp or even insects on my pages, so that's a bit of a disappointment.

To be honest, I still don't understand who these Forest Fringe people are. From what I can glean, I'm not actually a book about trees, but about moments. Moments a bit like the trees in Idaho, that lived for ten years exactly, or like the trees in Surrey, that were spindly and hard to fell. And not just moments, but "had to be there" moments. Which I sort of understand – when someone reads me, for example, like now, while you're reading me right now, this is a bit of a "had to be there" moment, isn't it, between you and I? Like this particular page – me – made up of infinitesimally small fragments of trees and pulp and thousands of newspapers and other books and paper towels and cardboard and processes that lead to this page just as it is – and you – your eyes, your brain, all the pulp that makes you up, that makes you just as you are, and all the books and newspapers and paper towels that lead to you being where you are and who you are right now. And now you're sat here reading me, with your mind and your attention just as it is right now. There's something nice about that, isn't there. Is that what this Forest Fringe thing is all about? Not trees, but moments? I'm still not sure, to be honest. I'm just glad that someone is interested enough in all that stuff to actually pick me up.

'60 seconds to mean what you say

This is an invitation to everyone to stand up and say something.

You have one minute to share your manifesto, your thoughts, feelings, demands for our future.'

Lucy Ellinson
One Minute Manifestos
2010

Lucy Ellinson has been involved with Forest Fringe from some of its earliest days, as an artist, as a friend, as a voice of fierce hope and compassion. One minute manifestos was perhaps the project that embodied that hope and compassion most fully. Anyone was invited to stand up and say something for one minute. If you agreed to do so Lucy would make a miniature stage for you on the bare floor out of tape. A small white square only a foot or so across, but enough to honour you, to provide you with space, both literal and figurative, in which to speak.

The manifestos took place on the crowded staircase on Bristo Place where people would wait to enter the venue. From out of the bustle of people queuing, drinking and talking these miniature performances would suddenly appear, and people would listen, and cheer, and often volunteer to be the person to go next.

I remember in particular one person, a volunteer at the venue, who used his minute not to say anything but instead to invite everyone to be quiet. A moment of blissful collective silence in the otherwise furious noise of the festival. It was one of the fondest memories I have of those early years at Forest Fringe.

I want to say that I think we should all try and take a bit more time in our lives, should slow down, look up and breath in.

I want to have that feeling of lying flat back on the grass and seeing the vastness of the sky but also feeling very present, connected to the soil – aware of your weight. Alive and awake. I think we should all wake up and look around a bit more. Start to see things. Give space to ideas we have but dismiss because maybe we think it would take too long. I think we should all make room in our lives for the point-less and the joyful – I think we should shake ourselves down, just dare to let go of what is driving us for a minute and breath out.

Write a letter instead of sending an email.

Walk instead of getting the train.

Pick up the phone instead of sending a text.

Go to a place you love and stand still for as long as you can, **look around and drink the world in**.

—— Shelley ——

This is a true story.

Two friends stand admiring something.

I am not actually sure what they are admiring.
I think that it is a building – a Gothic Cathedral,
stone arches, buttresses and towers soaring.

Perhaps it is a machine, or an engine.
I know that one of the friends likes vehicles.

It could equally be a painting,
maybe something by Pollock
or Picasso's Guernica or anything
by Paula Rego. Or a sculpture
– perhaps the figures
on Crosby beach.

Let's say that it is a building. And they are admiring it.

The first friend says, "It's amazing, isn't it,
to think that this was built by ordinary people."

"Yes, but," says the second friend,
"everything is done by ordinary people."

— Alex —

I believe that the world is fundamentally corrupt. And when I say the world I don't mean our communities. When I say the world I mean institutions – any institution – because I believe that the moment that people and lives are made into something that can easily be filed away onto a piece of paper they are not people, they are pieces of paper, and pieces of paper are easy to dispose of, to disappoint, to misfile.

I believe that the only truly beautiful things I own are gifts. I do not believe in buying gifts for myself. But I do believe in ensuring my own survival.

I believe that advertising makes it virtually impossible to be a good person or to do the right thing – I believe we are being constantly exposed to easy options, that we are trapped in a system that does not serve human beings – not good human beings, not bad human beings, in truth it serves no one. And I believe that the people who argue that this is incorrect know that they are lying to themselves. And are not truly happy with what is easy.

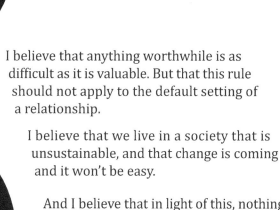

I believe that anything worthwhile is as difficult as it is valuable. But that this rule should not apply to the default setting of a relationship.

I believe that we live in a society that is unsustainable, and that change is coming and it won't be easy.

And I believe that in light of this, nothing is more important than kindness. You will only meet so many people in your life, even if you are aware of these very big, very confusing things. I believe in caring about each other.

I believe we are all at bottom compassionate people who want to build together, who want to work together, who want to care together.

There is a very annoying man next to me who is challenging this belief. But I'm doing my best. I believe in doing your best. He just apologized. I believe he meant it.

— Deborah —

The world's going to shits. Ruins. All down the drain. At least, that's what it looks like to me. And what can we do about it?

"Fucking nothing," is what I hear a lot for an answer.

I disagree. Strongly.

What's art got to do with the downfall of the world? Everything, I'd say. We're all enacting stories. Every day, all the time. Because it's part of the human condition, because we need them as much as air and food. What else is art than a form of dealing with the world and our lives in it?

Basically it's like this: we depend on heart-wrenching, thought-provoking, visionary stories and world views, told and presented by passionate, fierce performers, writers and artists. That might actually be the only chance we've got. All of us, whether so-called professionals or not. Because in society as a social sculpture as Joseph Beuys called it, **we're all artists. And desperately needed**

— Isa —

I HAVE NO INTEREST IN TELLING YOU WHAT ANYTHING IS. I HAVE NO INTEREST IN TELLING YOU WHAT I THINK IS RIGHT OR WRONG. THE ONLY THINGS THAT EXIST ARE ENERGY, AMBITION, AND THE DETERMI-NATION NOT TO LET YOURSELF DOWN BY WALKING AWAY BEFORE THE JOB IS DONE.

DO NOT GIVE UP

DO NOT LEAVE YOUR IDEAS HALF-BORN.

DO NOT WALK AWAY

BECAUSE OTHERWISE THE ONLY ONES LEFT GOING FORWARD ARE THE CUNTS OF THIS WORLD. AND IF WE GIVE UP AND FADE INTO THE BACKGROUND, THEIR VOICES WILL BE LOUD AND THEIR SIGNAL WILL BE ON ALL THE FREQUENCIES.

DO NOT STOP.

DO NOT STOP.

OR THEY WILL WIN.

— Chris —

'The deed is everything,
the glory naught. (Goethe)'

'This is the Gift Manifesto.

We live in an age of rampant capitalism.

An age when the laws of the market pervade our
every interaction – financial, political, social, personal.

An age when we can understand our relationship
with the world only in terms of value and return.

When all is reduced to a commodifiable transaction.

There is no alternative, no escape, because this is not simply
a system that surrounds us, it is one that we embody,
and perpetuate with nearly every thought and gesture.

In such an age the gift is a radical gesture.
A tiny rupture in our understanding of the world.
A space opened up to think differently.
To exist differently. To relate to each other differently.

Giving is a revolutionary act.
But we have forgotten how to give properly.
So this manifesto is a guide.
A guide to radical giving.

Do not do unto other as you would have them
do unto you. This is not giving it is a transaction.

Do not pay it forward. This is not giving, it is a balance sheet.

Do not give to those in need of your gift.
Those who will suffer without it.
This is not giving, this is common decency.
Just Give.   Give.   Give indiscriminately
Give often   Give when nobody asked
Give when nobody expected

Give in the unlikeliest of circumstances
Give to the unlikeliest of recipients
Give to those who don't want your gift.
Give anonymously
Give recklessly

Give when it inconveniences you
Give when it pains you
Give in imaginative, radical, impossible ways.
Give in ways that don't even look like giving.

Gestures become strategies become ways of living.
A few well placed gifts could change the world.'

—— Andy ——

Maybe If You Choreograph Me,

Tania El Khoury

Maybe If You Choreograph Me... was the third piece of one-to-one performance that Tania El Khoury had made with Forest Fringe and the most challenging by far for both audience and performer. It was a piece for a single male audience member, who would stand in a second floor window and choreograph by radio Tania's movements on the busy street below.

You Will Feel Better

2011

Maybe If You Choreograph Me...
is a piece about power and
representation. It recognises
both how power is performed
and how performance as an
artform participates in the
reproduction and maintenance
of structures of power. Even the
show's presence in our programme,
or any programme, is an act of
subversion – challenging us to
acknowledge who participates
in the making of that programme
and who is excluded from it. It is
this kind of provocation, both
through her work and through
her presence as a thinker and
contributor, that has made Tania
such an invaluable part of Forest
Fringe since she first began working
with us in 2009.

Now that you have given me my instructions, I will perform to you. And I will sing to you. Once I've passed by your window, I will be gone forever. However, when I pass by and take down my headphones, I want you to step out by opening the window from the top. You have the choice to shout out my name or to watch me disappear in silence. This will be your final decision.

Context
and Facts

• *Maybe If You Choreograph Me, You Will Feel Better* is a one-on-one performance created in 2011. This was a year of change on many fronts.

• In 2011, millions of people took to the streets across different Arab countries challenging authoritarian regimes by demanding accountability, transparency, and social justice.

• In 2011, activists occupied public squares around the world while branding capitalism and neoliberal policies unfair and unjust systems that exclusively benefit the rich and powerful.

• In 2011, riots erupted in England after police shot and killed 29-year-old Mark Duggan.

• 2011 was the last year that Forest Fringe happened in the old Forest building, where a community of anarchists and artists ran a performance venue and café before losing a battle to hold onto the building.

• *Maybe If You Choreograph Me, You Will Feel Better* won two awards during the 2011 Edinburgh Festival: the Arches Brick Award and the Total Theatre Innovation Award.

• During my speech in the first award ceremony, I talked about losing the only free venue during the Edinburgh Festival and called for both open borders and the opening up of art festivals to the political mobilizations that were occurring around us.

• After the award ceremony, someone told me that I should giggle and say "thank you" during award ceremonies instead of making political statements.

• During the second award ceremony, I publically thanked my boyfriend at the time for being "so shit that he inspired this work." The audience giggled.

• ***Maybe If You Choreograph Me, You Will Feel Better*** is not really about my ex-boyfriend. Though the idea came to me after listening to his endless choreographic instructions in the kitchen.

• The show was only to self-identifying male audience members. As a one-on-one show, the man was the spectator as well as the collaborator in the performance.

• The Battersea Arts Centre in London commissioned the show for their one-on-one festival.

- **The Guardian's art critic Lyn Gardner questioned** via Twitter how come the show was only for men.

- In response, I wrote a blog post arguing that in creating temporary relationships as performances, we should be able to choose our audience-collaborators like they choose us. Because these relationships need to work for us too as artists.

- Gardner then wrote an article on the subject titled "Do Theatre Audiences Really Decide What Shows They See?"

- **The idea of the show** is to give a man (audience) who is standing behind a third-floor window the perfect scene of a woman (performer) passing by his window.

- For this to happen, the man needed to create everything about me: my name, my movements, and even my feelings.

- The man hears a pre-recorded voice in the room he's standing in. It lets him know that I'm outside and that he can talk to me through a dictaphone and I can hear him through a pair of wireless headphones. There is no way for me to talk back.

- The voice in the pre-recorded message is not mine. It is the beautiful voice of Laura Whitticase who at the very end of the performance delivers a song, which stays with you for a long time.

- Passers-by in the street often became accidental audiences, collaborators, or participants.

- ***In Edinburgh, I allowed*** a woman to listen to the piece from another window without participating in the piece.

- The woman liked the experience so much and ever since we've opened the show for one woman in each show to watch the piece happen from another window or room.

- **The piece toured** across nine cities in eight different countries. Since it is a one-on-one show, it had to be repeated a few times a day often in a row.

- I only later realized that I devised a full performance show for one audience member. I did not think about the touring aspect of it or how I would need to repeat it many times a day.

- I was told that my show was an economical disaster.

- I fought to set a limit of a maximum of four shows in a row.

- On some days, even one show was too many.

- I started drinking whiskey shots before each performance.

- **During the show, I performed** whatever the audience instructed me to do. This included running into a wall, punching the pavement, collapsing on the ground, and jumping in front of a moving car.

- The police stopped me during the show on three occasions in different countries for looking suspicious in the streets.

- In Toronto, a man sexually harassed me while I was performing the piece.

- In Edinburgh, a group of kids racially harassed me while I was performing the piece.

- In London, an audience member came back to see the show the next day after participating in it the first day. He spent the duration of the performance bullying me.

- In Glasgow, I had to have a "security" person with me in the streets and agree on secret signs that would reveal that I'm in trouble.

- In Ljubljana and Dublin, I bumped into friends while performing. It was awkward.

- In Lisbon, an older woman thought I was troubled and gave me a very tender hug. I felt touched but also guilty.

- In Toronto, I fell in love with an audience member.

• **To my surprise, I discovered** in the recordings that many audience members cry at the end of the piece when I disappear into the crowd.

• One audience member left a message saying he never felt as close to anyone before. Though I was an imaginary character with no voice.

• What audience members opened up to was their own gender politics. The choices they made as well as the inspirations they drew on in creating my character were very telling.

• **I stopped touring** the piece. It was always tiring, often frustrating, and sometimes depressing.

• When do we stop touring interactive performances that were meant to function as social experiments? Do we tour them as long as they are in demand or do we stop after being satisfied (or not) by the results?

• *I was frustrated (though not surprised)* by the behaviour of many of the male audience members who abused the power they were granted over my body and presence in the streets. I was also disappointed by some of the women's responses to the show.

• Some colleagues or fellow feminists suggested that the piece represents the oppression of Arab women in Arab countries. The burden of representing millions that artists of colour still need to deal with is sickening.

• *On a personal, political, and artistic level*, 2011 was tiring, scary, exciting and very much felt like jumping into the mouth of a beast. A whole generation of people seems to have suffered insomnia from too much excitement that year. It was unhealthy to sustain the practice, but many of us would do anything to relive those very moments.

brief

Gemma

Brockis

2012

2012 was an unusual year for Forest Fringe. The previous year had been our last on Bristo Place, after our friends and hosts the Forest Café were forced from their home when their landlords went into administration.

The next year would be our first at the Out of the Blue Drill Hall and the beginning of a new chapter.

For now, however, we were neither place. Without a bricks and mortar home for our artists we decided instead, with the support of Jerwood Charitable Foundation, to create a venue made from paper and ink – a festival of performances contained within the pages of a book handed out for free to people at the festival.

We called this temporary home Paper Stages, and gave each contributing artists a double page spread in which to create a performance.

Gemma Brockis' short play for two people was a beautiful contribution to the festival and a perfect example of the beguiling strangeness of this format. It is neither entirely read or entirely performed. Neither entirely real or entirely imagined. It exists in the space between your eyes and the page. In the sound of the voices speaking the lines in your head. It creates for itself a space of uncertainty, a moment of tenderness and a kind quiet loneliness so rarely possible in live performance.

In the following little play, **you play you.**
I play I.

It is a two-hander.
Do not concern yourself
with being typecast. **You are not.**

All you have to do is speak
your part aloud. Choose a
location where this won't
be a problem. There is no
need to project your voice.
I will be very close by. Even
if you whisper, I will hear.
In fact, a whisper works
well for the character. **And take your time.**

You will speak and I will
respond in the moment to
just how you have spoken
– your tone of voice, the
speed at which your lips
move, the tilt of your head.
The way you speak to me
will change everything.

BRIEF

A play by Gemma Brockis

After the novel of the same name

A room. We can hear sound from the surroundings, but it is as though muffled. As the action continues the walls of the room should seem to grow further apart, so that eventually they disappear into the distance, giving the impression that we are in fact outside, looking at exterior walls. At the same time, the stage gradually become overgrown with shrubbery so that it is reminiscent of a park, or a hillock. It could be anywhere.

As the curtain rises, the atmosphere is pleasingly banal, only interrupted by a small invisible bird that occasionally circles in the air somewhere above the action. The overall effect is indescribably appealing yet ominous. You are sitting centre stage, reading a book.

YOU.

YOU.

YOU.

YOU.

YOU.

YOU.

(*very intimate*). It's you.

>Pause.

You again.

>Pause.

Can you hear me?

>*I am strangely silent. Elusive.*

(*certain*). You can hear me.

>*I remain still and silent. But I nevertheless have a very effective stage presence.*

What's going on? (*Serious.*) I mean. Between us.

>*Responding to your tone, I look at you suddenly. I am scrutinising your expression. But you don't look back. You will never look at me throughout the course of the play.*

It can't go on like this.

>*I say nothing but I am thinking about you. You are so far away.*

Well?

YOU.

YOU.

YOU.

I open my mouth as if to say, 'long distance relationships are notoriously difficult', but I stop myself before the words form.

You don't want to talk about it?

I don't.

Pause.

In a moment, when the music starts, you will gaze into the distance, not really seeing anything, but listening for a while, before returning to the page.

SOUND CUE: SLOW BLUES PIANO DRIFTS IN FROM THE DISTANCE.

Pause.

We have to talk about it.

I shudder at the thought. I know I'm not up to the task.

My friends say you are a coward.

I look at you. But you still refuse to meet my gaze, staring steadfastly into the page. I keep my eyes fixed on you while I mouth words so clearly that, though you cannot hear them, you sense them.

I.

YOU.

YOU.

YOU.

YOU.

I AM A COWARD. THAT'S WHY I HAVEN'T COME. I CAN'T BEAR THE THOUGHT OF ACTUALLY SITTING IN THE SAME ROOM WITH YOU EVEN THE SAME PARK WITH YOU WITHOUT TOUCHING YOU I DON'T KNOW IF I COULD STOP MYSELF AND I DON'T KNOW IF YOU'D LIKE ME IF I DIDN'T STOP. I DON'T KNOW IF MY TOUCH ON YOUR CHEEK WOULD RESULT IN YOU GRASPING MY HAND AND KISSING IT HARD, OR IF YOU WOULD SHRUG ME OFF, LIKE A FLY OR A SHARP PAIN, OR PERHAPS YOU WOULD GO SO FAR AS TO WRITE A LETTER OF COMPLAINT TO THE GOVERNMENT. IS IT TAXPAYERS' MONEY THAT ENABLES MY HAND TO REST SILENTLY ON YOUR SOFT CHEEK FOR AN INSTANT? HOW CAN THAT BE JUSTIFIED? HOW CAN I JUSTIFY THAT? WHEN IT GIVES ME SUCH PLEASURE?

> *Silence.*

You can't touch me.

> *Silence.*

I can touch you.

> *Hopeful silence.*

Because you are here.

> *Doubtful silence.*

I can sense it because of your effective stage presence. Look...

YOU.

Without looking up, you point your finger gingerly in front of you. As you do so, I step toward you. My body slips around your finger, so that it is now embedded in between my ribs just below my heart. Wind in the trees.

You are warm.

We stay like this for a short while. Above us, the bird circles continually.

the end

Sam Halmarack

Songs

and the Miserablites

2013

Once of the first trips for the show outside of Bristol was to the Forest Fringe takeover at The Gate Theatre. I was convinced it was the kind of show that would fit in a suitcase. Hauling a stadium-sized hazer on the many flights of stairs on underground that day, I discovered it wasn't. So keen was I for the show to be a success at Forest, my girlfriend of the time drove up from Bristol with some extra PA speakers to reinforce the sound. And it was a success.

Performing the following year at Forest Fringe in Edinburgh, we had night after night of joy-filled singalongs. I'm still touring the show three years later. The age gap between hopeful rehearsal DVD guide and jaded performer growing all the time. The show wouldn't have been made without close friends, most notably Kate Yedigaroff and the Ferment artist development initiative at the Bristol Old Vic and it wouldn't have connected to audiences without the unique, suitcase-destroying wonder that is Forest Fringe.

Those that are broken hearted take faith...
This isn't wasted time or a wasted life
It's just a long, long way
If you've written off your chance of making it
Think straight
Our day in the sunshine is coming to justify
these years of rain

Everything happens for a reason ... everything

If you've tried everything you can think of, try again

Put your hand into my hand and together we'll find a way

What doesn't kill us makes us stronger every day

Soon we'll have superhuman strength enough to show the world
we deserve our day.

To be champions of the universe

Everything happens for a reason... everything

'Champions Of The Universe'

'I Never Was Been'

They say that I'm past it
They say that I"m done
I'm 30 something
Still not number one
but the way to the top is a long winding road
just 'cause we're living in the fast lane,
it's the same distance to go

> I'm not a has been
> because I never was been
> but you know I think I might be
> for just this moment

It's been years of this hardship
overworked, underpaid
but through all the struggles
our spirit has stayed
I'm gonna undo my seatbelt

move from the passenger seat
life's not something to run from,
it's something to beat

Join and clap

I'm not a has been
because I never was been
but you know I think I might be
for just this moment

Everybody thinks they're
special and they're right
but you're all gonna make me
feel special tonight

**Hands in the air. Look intense.
Join in with the verse this time.**

They say that I'm past it
They say that Im done
I'm 30 something
Still not number one
but the way to the top is a long
winding road
just 'cause we're living in the fast
lane, it's the same distance to go

Join in and clap

I'm not a has been
because I never was been
but you know I think I might be
for just this moment

You don't ask for much
You don't ask for much from us

We are the champions
of the universe

They don't expect us to win,
why don't we surprise them all

before we've even
spoken a word

**'We Are The Champions
of The Universe'**

'This Is Romance'

Fuck all your whistles
and fuck all your bells

and those white
flashing lights you can
fuck them as well

rather go quiet than
be insincere

rather be alone than
be with anybody here

and when they all clap their
hands we will sneak out the back

Fuck your funny stories
and your great tattoos
Fuck your Facebook tags
and your MySpace views

Rather be strange
than straight with you
The best things all happen
when the party is through

and when they all clap their hands
we will sneak out the back

This is romance

'We Are Not Giving Up'

We are not giving up
We travelled millions of miles to be here
we are not giving up
We are not giving up

Nobody can stop us now
We are a billion strong and building
Nobody can stop us now

You can tire us out, you can tire us out,
you can tire us out, you can tire us out...

We are standing proud
We're standing up for what we believe in
We are all standing proud
We are all standing proud

We have let go of doubt
You can tell we were born to be leaders
There's no harm in standing out

You can tire us out, you can tire us out,
you can tire us out, you can tire us out...
You can tire us out, you can tire us out,
you can tire us out, you can tire us out...
but we're still going to be here

Three in the back, two in the front.
This is how ride when we're going to a concert

put

your sweet hand

Andy Field & Ira Brand
2014

in mine

put your sweet hand in mine is a show about love and the many different things we might mean when we talk about love. It is a show for 40 people sat in two rows facing one another. As they sit, close enough that they could hold hands should they wish, we tell them stories about their imagined relationships to one another. We tell them they are in Paris, or in Antarctica, or lost in the middle of a thunderstorm. We ask them to look, sometimes awkwardly, into the eyes of the stranger sat opposite them and to imagine a love for that person that shifts and reforms with each passing scene.

The following pages do not contain the full text of the piece, or any explicit descriptions of the staging. Instead we have tried to use some of the original words to create a sketch of each scene, like a series of model boxes or the kind of half-remembered traces you might retain had you experienced the actual performance.

put your sweet hand in mine was created with James Stenhouse, Beckie Darlington and Gemma Brockis, with the support of Battersea Arts Centre, ARC Stockton Arts Centre and Arts Council England.

Scene 1
the theatre

near darkness
anticipation
shuffling
two performers
two microphones

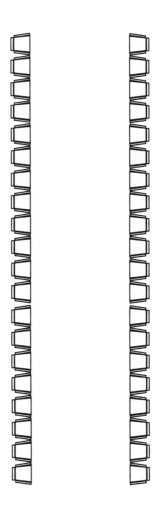

Anticipation
and the gentle fizz of overburdened
electrical equipment
A ballet of shuffles in the almost
darkness
the show
it would seem
is about to start
Silence
and a collaborative attempt at
concentration
no more chattering voices
faded out like the end of an old song
But nothing is happening
yet
An apologetic cough
seems to give your eyes permission to
shuffle conspicuously down the aisle
like two latecomers taking their seats
You admire a chorus line of hands and
knees
some still some nervous
some feverishly tapping on mobile
phones
some flexing and stretching like it is
they that are about to take the stage
You wonder
as you always do
who any of these people are
you have no history yet
nothing in common
Until something happens
you are not quite yet an audience

Scene 2
A Lecture on the Bird Life of Paris

projector screen
distracting images
babble
birds
the suggestion of rain

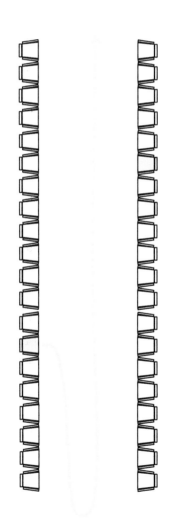

...llo everyone. Thanks very much for making it, it's lovely to see so many new faces. I hope ... ade ... , th ... j ... troduc ... ... o so ... ... y seem ... rribly b ... but ... e c ... be wit ... e and I p ... mise ... ings ... g ... more exciting ... xt we ... en v ... tu ... l ... e a ... nce to ... out ... th ... ... ulars and ... pro ... ick S ... re ... be ... The firs ... ace ... ... lways with a map ... re ... ... or y ... ne ... f ... n. Be wa ... ed th ... gh, th ... k ... centuries o ... ench ... ndsc ... e ... garder ... g ... these par ... are b ... on l ... ns ... on wi ... ness meaning you won't find much beyond those birds you'd expect to see in any ... northern Eu ... ci ... p ... ... There are however, ... v places that ... e excep ... ns ... ou coul ... o wors ... nan st ... with the Père Lachaise ... metery for e ... mple. A ... nd ... d acre ... f arbor ... l garde ... that are most famou ... the resting p ... e of su ... ro ... lu ... ies ... Oscar ... lde and Marcel Prous ... re amongst t ... trees th ... gs ... rt to g ... a little m ... e interes ... ng. Listen carefully and ... u can expect ... th ... fa ... ar call ... he Gre ... te ... dpecker who, like ... ust, is a year-round resident, his mosaic of white and black feathers topped with ... extravagant red flourish making him one of the best dressed characters in the ... ghbourhou ... e G ... tte W ... dpe ... er ... ... another of Paris ... dsome bac ... ors, ... mat ... fo fe ... c pk ... naking ... nor for themselve ... ether in the c ... mete ... es talk ... tre ... n ... ve ... gre ... al is another life ... ter, the Eura ... n W ... dhat ... an ... eir ... y s ... bbling ... one ... f the first thing ... u should be lis ... ning c ... ne c ... e b ... hin ... t ... eme ... ry like this is the ... nce; the lack of traffic, the sound only of the crunch of gravel under people's fee ... d the occasional whispered prayer or anecdote. Head up the small covered trail ... the north, listen c ... ng ... ... k able to ... ar the familiar call of the ... ropean Robin an ... ossibly if t ... re lu ... y ... sound ... f a Eurasian Wren; a high ... eathless, jittering tw ... hat ca ... es in ... like an ... carrier bag. Many people ... em to think birdsong is ... abo ... court ... p, ... ich, wl ... t very romantic is sadly in ... rect. Birds sing fo ... es ... of re ... ns. T ... t ... t ... me ... To defend their territory o ... rn others away. Some birds sing whilst in flight. Others sing as the sun rises. Re ... rchers in Costa Rica, found that a dawn chorus of Banded Wrens involved severa ... le ... ver ... actually li ... ar res ... ndi ... to ne ... oth ... n co ... ways ... pira ... ing ut of lo ... ness ... r ... st ... to ... n ... l ... en S ... e si ... g as ar ... y or as c ... y for h ... o. So ... s ... ... ir th ... re ... v ... f ... tionships o ... mi ... t. ... er bec ... ing s ... ar ... fr ... eir ... ik ... n. ... e s ... g h ... g los ... eli ... d. ... eir pla ... n f ... worl ... eep ... in s, ... ave ... spa ... he ... oms ... ging ... o anyo ... e that will list ... ... Finding comp ... ions ... p fr ... m the ... nlike ... t ... f birds. ... u continue to follow the trails northwards you'll find yourself in the park's most fertile ... for l ... esp ... ally ... the ... igra ... y ... Wait t ... ar ... Nove ... be ... n t ... ec ... s a ... alli ... ar ... ne ... iris ... have ... ge ... one and ... s ... d b ... ble ... t ... m ... ne ... e ... ir ... irdlife. A ... tteri ... of s ... g thrush ... irs ... or ... nor ... ic ... ch ... hif ... af ... ific ... s ... ng ... e ground ... e ... k ... se ... lia ... r ... t th ... ov ... s ... d qu ... r ... ks co ... ting ... ound Jir ... o ... on. ... d ... , if ... u tir ... it ... t rig ... e ir ... ossib ... clou ... s expan ... at ... e yo ... jou ... catch a glimpse of a Eurasian Hobby, *Falco subbuteo*, a wiry little falcon speed ... ating through the dusk ... blu ... like ... dying ... atellit ... like ... message from some othe ... mension. But let me be ... w ... t wit ... you. It ... nc ... or ... em that I come here. I'm no ... tually all that interested in th ... dom ... ic sa ... ok ... n of the woodpeckers or the alier ... auty of the falcons. I wait c ... wai ... ... l ... ntil craning my neck I can see ... ouetted against the fading ... ght a ... ck of ... rc ... an Greenfinch, each bird a single ... rely audible syllable in an e ... lessl ... ewrit ... p ... t spills up into the sky like a ... ebration, now moving, over my head and beyond the cemetery gates, blocking ... ds stopping traffic no longer one or another, finding strength not in the muscle o ... y ... g ... ir ... irg ... a ... of ... shar ... mov ... ne ... g ... ma ... s, co ... v ... lin ... ast metro ... ations ... irat ... s, ... d ... round ... ce sirens ... argu ... g ... ers, ... them ... ves ... d in ... e ... ishly flap ... ings ... . Th ... ks ... ry ... much ... r list ... ng. ... s ... m ... fr ... all of ... o ... ere nex ... d if ... ... ag ... ing t ... jo ... pleas ... e ... emt ... o ... ... oc ... ... 'll be ... ng out whatever the weather.

Scene 3
Paris metro

the rattle of train carriages
awkward eye contact
brief flights of fancy

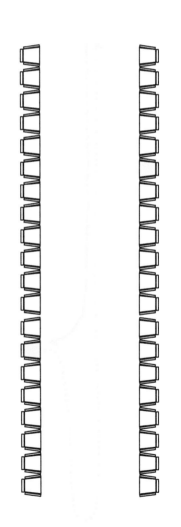

IRA	ANDY

ANDY: Sorry, have we met?

IRA: *You want to smile but you stop yourself. You say, calmly:* the Salle Pleyel.

ANDY: When?

IRA: A few weeks back.

ANDY: You work there?

IRA: No.

ANDY: Did we sit together?

IRA: No.

ANDY: Are you sure?

IRA: Yes. We just, um, we just we just sort of looked at each other a few times I guess.

ANDY: Oh.

IRA: We smiled.

ANDY: I remember. Sure. That was a great concert.

IRA: Really great.

ANDY: I remember you.

IRA: Yeah. Yeah. I remember.

pause

Scene 4
antarctic

total darkness
radio static
wind
the suggestion of ice

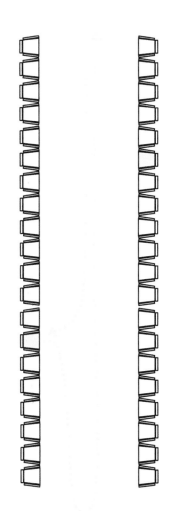

In the darkness
You trace a safe path along an outer ridge
The landscape tremors as you place your feet on it.
It murmurs pleasure and unrest.
The ground is frozen water packed solid
Snow stacked and stacked and compressed and then
succumbed to the pull of gravity
Like any river to the sea.
Metal crampons are clamped and pulled taught like jaws
on to the soles of your boots
The teeth of the metal hold you fast on to his her body.
This is what is known as the terminal face.
The glacier's front
Its fingertips outstretched.
Up on the spine of the glacier you find new holes where
the melt has spread
It is changing constantly
So slowly you don't see it
But sometimes whole metres in a day
The terminal face recedes.
She he shifts colour as you rotate and the sun rotates
As you blink their eyes seem to change colour in front of
you
Now dark now light now dark again
Like a magic trick.

Deeper in the valley, the ice forms into a palisade of
tight peaks.
A landscape pulling itself up as if inhaling
Peaks and spits, becoming lips, clefts, ridges, crinkles of
skin
The tip of a vulva, or the sharp fold between mons and
hip joint.

In the centre of the valley
At the glacier's widest
Whitest
Point
It resembles a dream you once had

Of Antarctica.

Of pulling ourselves forwards on sleds
As they pitch on a frozen ocean
Righting our bodies with the last remnants of strength
To catch a pioneer's glimpse of the whiteness
And arrive at this new world with good posture

A violent air on the back of your throat as you inhale.
800 miles away from open sea
Just snow, ice, and six months of daytime

Your skin is charred at the extremities
And your blood is slow
Some days you doubt whether your eyes are still working
properly
Whether your vision has become stunted by lack of
variety
Whether your heart has shrunk like astronauts in space
Except we haven't been to space yet
And the word astronaut does not exist.

You are hungry all the time
And when you stop being hungry
This is when you know that you are dying.

You pull yourself forward on your feet
Two and a half thousand metres of solid ice flesh
You walk upon her him
The word 'vast' forms on the tip of your/my tongue
But vast is a word both inadequate and too much

To take it in, all of the bigness
To gather it in your arms
To harness it in some way, plant a flag
To circumscribe it, like a globe
Or an ocean
Your tongue licking up sea spray and snow and sweat
and meteorite dust
That is why you are here.
You have dreamt of being the first
Though you couldn't quite explain why it's so important
But in this age there is always another man woman who
has been there first

A flag whips
Norwegian
A small dark tent sits lopsided
Held on all sides taught by strings
Weighted down by the snow recently fallen or blown by
the wind
You can't be sure
You couldn't care really
Except it means that they were here

Fucking Amundsen
Fucking ice fucking snow fucking wind and windburn
Fucking sunburn without the pleasure ever of warmth
Fuck fuck fuck

A flag whips
In your hand
We will place it here anyway
We will have to place it somewhere
On the skin inside of an upper arm
On the rise of an Achilles' tendon
We will find somewhere to mark as our own
It won't be the obvious places
The cunts and breasts and cocks and arses
Or the eyes the lips the small of the back
It will be the place we least expected to fall in love with
The unsymmetrical bottom edge of their nose
The protruding mole
The bowl of a burnt-out tree.

When you come to it is dark
And if anything
It is colder
There is still no suggestion of when the power might be
restored
You are just a body
Outlined against another body
The heat of your breath
Warming the space between you
Your breath mingling.
Obscuring distinct lines
Between the inside and outside
The warm spaces and the cold.

Scene 5
a kidnapping

melting ice
cold hands
more uncomfortable staring

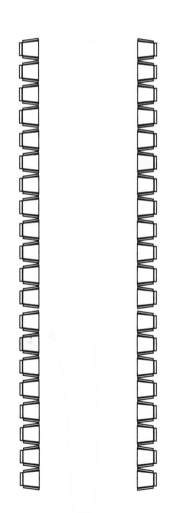

People are forgetting who I am.

                                    I know who you are.

Other people are probably forgetting who I am.
I am forgetting who I am.

                              What do you want me to say?

You've stolen all my good ideas.
All my youthful energy.
The best years of my life.

                              I haven't taken anything.

Why are you always holding me?

                              It's what I'm supposed to do.

You're making me feel very uncomfortable
Like a caged bird.

                                    We're a team.

Like a canary.

                    We've got a lot invested in this.

Scene 6
preacherman

anxious pacing
God Only Knows
yet more symbolic birds

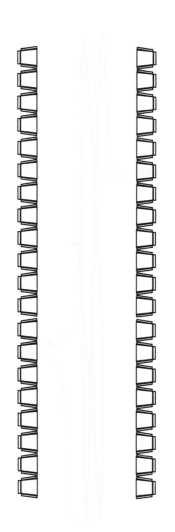

Or a bar
Or you just sit in the front seat of your car
wondering what the fuck I'm doing with my life

And then just when you think it might all be getting
too much, For no particular reason
And it's not that you've been drinking
Maybe it's church bells or something
But actually you're not feeling alone any more

You're just feeling ready
You know
Ready for something strange
Ready for something you don't already know the
shape of
You are ready to open your heart
You don't need any other birds any more
Or a nest or
You don't need anyone
You are finally ready
And you open your throat
And you say

Please
Take me to the promised land
and I don't care if that's
Jerusalem
or Paris
or a sandwich board that says
we can be saved
that says
everything might be ok
that says
I am ready to love again
that says
Hey
you up there
give me a sign

Pause

I said give me a sign

Pause

155

Pl

Scene 7
a storm

I Want To Know What Love Is
wet clothes
rain
shouting

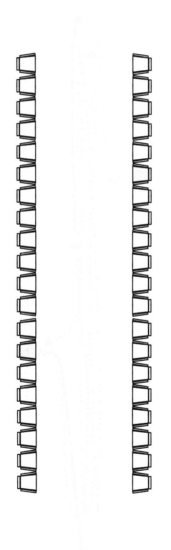

WHY
DIDN'T YOU
WRITE ME?

I WROTE
YOU EVERY
DAY FOR A
YEAR.

I'm not walking away from this.

Sorry isn't good enough.

Where would we go?
I never meant to lie to you.

Is it still raining? I hadn't noticed.

You can. And you will.

We'll just have to use our hands.

You have to throw me the rope!

You've got to get on that plane!

Go back. Save yourself.

Just hand me the gun.

If this bomb goes off then we're going with it.

Why can't you be more specific about things?

It's too late.

It's too steep.

It hurts.
Why won't somebody help us?

I'm sorry!

I'm sorry!

You're going to have to jump!

What about all these people?

They don't have anyone.

I just wanted to tell you I'm sorry.

We've got to get out of here.

This kind of weather really scares the animals.

It's not safe out here.

I can't do this anymore.

There's no electricity.

Go back! It's too dangerous.

I can't reach it.

I never asked for any of this.

I'm not leaving here until you speak to me.

If this boat goes down then I'm going with it.

I don't know how much longer I can hold on.

I can't see anything.

It's too far.

It's too hard.

This can't be the end.

I'm sorry!

I'm sorry!

I don't know if I can trust you.

They can take care of themselves!

They have each other.

Scene 8
coda

held hands
offstage microphone
absent performers

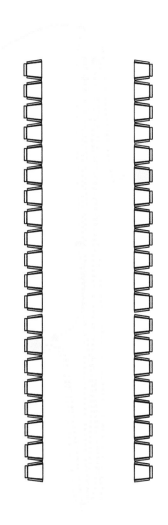

Hold on
We're nearly through this.
Hold on, you say to yourself like a
mantra
You say to them just with the pulse of
blood beneath the skin of your hand
You are just textures and temperatures
in the darkness
Germs and dirt and dust
Everything is most probably going to be
okay
Or if not okay
It will pass
It will be history
And we will still have this
Or a memory of this
A muscle memory
Of handshakes
And handholds
Greetings
Deals made
Truces
Apologies
A nod and shake before a big game
Clutching a hand beside you for the
first time in the darkness of a cinema
For the last time in a besieged building
In a car without breaks
The air steward reassuring at take-off
A doctor saying squeeze here for the
pain
Sweaty hands slipping apart at the
crest of a cliff
Or warming yourselves in each other's
pockets
And every arm wrestle ever
Love maybe
Probably love
And then just the feeling of holding
Or being held
Even if only temporarily.

SELINA THOMPSON

Race Cards

2015

Race Cards was supported by Buzzcut, Forest Fringe and Fierce FWD. Seed commissioned by Camden People's Theatre and Leeds Library through Room 700 with thanks to Msri Dey, Ria Hartley, Jo Bannon, Hannah Silva, Victoria Pratt, Bethany Wells and Jamal Gerald.

'*The Bluest Eye* was my effort to say something about that; to say something about why she had not, or possibly ever would have the experience of what she possessed and also why she prayed for so radical an alteration. Implicit in her desire was racial self-loathing. And twenty years later, I was still wondering about how one learns that. Who told her? Who made her feel that it was better to be a freak than what she was? Who had looked at her and found her so wanting, so small a weight on the beauty scale? The novel pecks away at the gaze that condemned her.

The reclamation of racial beauty in the sixties stirred these thoughts, made me think about the necessity for the claim. Why, although reviled by others, could this beauty not be taken for granted within the community? Why did it need wide public articulation to exist? These are not clever questions. But in 1962 when I began the story, and in 1965 when it began to be a book, the answers were not as obvious to me as they quickly become and are now. The assertion of racial beauty was not a reaction to the self-mocking, humorous critique of cultural/racial foibles common in all groups, but against the damaging internalization of assumption of immutable inferiority originating in an outside gaze.'

Toni Morrison, Foreword to *The Bluest Eye*

I'm Selina.

This is Race Cards, and I'm waiting inside this room for you.

This is the fourth time I've done Race Cards. It's a little different each time. My 'politics' has shifted, rapidly, in the past year. This work has to keep mutating to keep up.

This version is for me, and one other person at any one time.

Inside this room, I am writing 1000 questions about race. I'm writing them on little white cards. I am writing the questions so that they don't live in my body in quite the same way any more.

Enter the room, head to the back, and take as much time as is needed to read the questions and the answers you will see stuck on the walls there. Take your time.

If you want to enter this room, and read the questions, there's an exchange.

The exchange is in two parts.

1. You must answer a question. Write your answer using the red ink and fountain pen on the table, as well as the cards provided. When you have answered, stick the answer on the wall. Leave it in the space, with me. It is my answer to hold, a gift from you to me. Pick one that is difficult to answer.

2. Your final task is to copy a question from the wall onto a card of your own. Write it in the red ink, and take it from the space with you. It is your question to hold, a gift from me to you. Pick one you can't answer.

You may spend as long as you like in the room, reading questions, selecting which you will answer, and copying your question. I will be silent, and any exchange between us will only happen via the cards.

If you need any assistance in the room, or have any access requirements, please speak with Emma before entering and she will be able to assist you.

1. How do you go about exposing white supremacy in liberal arts spaces?

2. How do you go about exposing white supremacy in liberalism and the left in general?

3. When I say white supremacy, what do you think of?

4. And when I say white supremacy, what do you think I mean?

5. What to do once that white supremacy has been exposed?

Perhaps I have already gotten ahead of myself –

6. Do you think there is white supremacy in liberal arts spaces?

7. If there is, what does it mean for me to be here?

8. And what does it mean for you to be here too?

9. How do I negotiate your gaze?

10. What has shaped your gaze?

11. Who sees through the white gaze?

12. What is the opposite of the white gaze?

13. How do you feel when you hear (or say) the word 'diverse'?

14. Whatever happened to multiculturalism?

15. What is the purpose of language like this – diverse/ multicultural/BAME/ etc. etc.

16. Should I have jumped straight in with a white supremacy question, or given you some time to settle in first?

17. How does saying white supremacy instead of racism change the way a question is read?

18. Let's do some easy basics. What does it mean to be black?

19. And of course, what does it mean to be white?

20. What is meant by the term 'politically black'?

21. And what does it mean to be brown?

22. Or to be Jewish?

23. What does it mean for all the countries in a continent to be squished into one, amorphous label?

24. If my granddad was born in Jamaica, my nan was born in Montserrat, my other granddad was born in Ghana, as was my other Nan and both my parents were both here, but I'm adopted and both my biological parents who I've never met were born Jamaican, what's my ancestry?

25. At what age do children realise that they are black (if they are, of course)?

26. At what age do children realise they are white?

27. How do they deal with realising this?

28. When was the last time that you were aware of your race?

29. What happens if rather than focusing on solutions to racial tension, we approach them as immutable, unchangeable, just part of being human now?

30. What is the long-term psychological impact of white supremacy on people of colour?

31. What role should mental healthcare provision play in emancipatory politics?

32. Is immigration traumatic?

33. If trauma can be passed down genetically, what does that mean for the descendants of immigrants?

34. Are our definitions of trauma broad enough?

35. Are our definitions of violence broad enough?

36. What does it mean for me to 'reclaim' a country my descendants are from that I have never visited?

37. Where does that leave the people that live there now – especially if there is huge economic disparity between their country and mine?

38. What do people who trace their ancestry back expect to find?

39. How do you perceive race if you are blind?

40. How do you feel about the terms 'honky' and 'cracker'?

41. What is the work that I need to do, when my best friend – a gay black man – tells me that some of the most painful, homophobic interactions he has had have been with black women?

42. Where am I an oppressor in my daily life?

43. And where are you an oppressor in yours?

44. Are public intellectuals important?

45. Why is it so easy for these questions to slip into binary?

46. What is dangerous about us talking about race in terms of binary?

47. How do we keep ourselves from doing that?

48. How did the politics of binaries permeate the Exhibit B debate?

49. Where do these binaries leave people of dual ethnicity?

50. How do we critique one another with love?

51. How can I have all these questions in my head and remain soft, loving, gentle?

52. How do you stop the struggle becoming your identity?

53. What does it look like when 'the struggle' is your identity?

54. How do you let violence like that out of your body?

55. Do activists have higher rates of mental health problems?

56. How much work do you have to do before you get to self care?

57. What is your responsibility if there are racists in your family?

It feels like a good time to remind you that 'these are not clever questions'

58. What would be a clever question to ask about race?

59. Why is the language of family – 'brother', 'sister' – so prevalent in black liberatory activism?

60. What does this tell me about what people need from that kind of activism?

61. What is it to hear somebody say 'I Can't Breathe' – but to decide not to loosen the headlock?

62. I met a man who said his dad opened the first Indian corner shop on Thursday. Do you think he was telling the truth?

63. How do you cook plantain?

64. What does your bit of the diaspora call yam?

65. Do you eat Jollof from Nigeria or Ghana?

66. Why do we try to make stories about the history of black people feel like narratives of trajectory?

67. How far can non-violence get you when dealing with an oppressive state?

68. What is it to be militant?

69. Am I militant?

70. Is militancy and violence intrinsically united?

71. How do we ensure we look at the cause not the symptoms?

72. What does a world liberated for all look like?

73. Or do I simply need to create that in my house?

74. Do I really look like Jennifer Hudson?

75. Do I really look like Ella Fitzgerald?

76. Do I really look like Tastee from Orange is the New Black?

77. Do I really look like Viola Davis?

78. Do I really look like whoever the fat black girl is on X Factor this year?

79. Do I really look like the only other black woman that works here?

80. Do I really look like the other black woman over the other side of the restaurant?

81. Do I really look like the other little black girl from our brownies group?

82. Do I really look like the one other black girl in our halls?

83. Do I really look like a young Cicely Tyson?

84. Is the room you're in a safe space for you?

85. Is outside that room a safe space for you?

86. Is Forest Fringe a safe space for you?

87. Is outside the building you're in a safe space for you?

88. If I were to time travel, where in history would I be most safe?

89. What does a safe neighbourhood look like to you?

90. What is a safe space?

91. Is safe space ever truly possible?

92. Where do safe spaces exist in your life?

93. Do artists get to inhabit safe spaces?

94. Do activists get to inhabit safe spaces?

95. Does anybody have a right to a safe space?

96. When was the last time you were in a safe space, and what was it like?

97. Are there safe spaces for Straight White Men?

98. Are you lucky enough to be reading this at a time when we have grown bored of safe space discourse?

99. What would a brave space mean for conversation about race?

100.   I know that you're black –
but are you NEW BLACK?

101.   I know that you're black –
but maybe you're ONLY TECHNICALLY BLACK?

102.   I know that you're black –
but are you KUNTE KINTE BLACK?

103.   I know that you're black –
but are you BLACK BLACK?

104.   I know that you're black –
but are you ANGRY BLACK?

105. What were you expecting from a text called race cards?

106. What do you expect from a performance about race from a black woman?

107. And what would you expect from a performance about race from a white man?

108. What are our expectations of art made by people of colour?

109. What is the best way for artists of colour to negotiate Arts Industries in the UK?

110. What are the dangers of making art about race?

111. How can you negotiate these dangers?

112. Why is race politics automatically read as 'radical'?

113. And what does that radical mean?

114. What does the destruction of a mural of 'Sandra Bland' – the words 'All Lives Matter' painted all over it – tell me about the phrase 'All Lives Matter'?

115. How many Beyoncé tweets before people who thought you were radical hit 'unfollow'?

116. What damage is done by overuse of the word radical?

117. How do you respond to somebody telling you your politics is a 'brand'?

118. How can someone in the mainstream support someone on the fringes without co-option?

119. Is cultural appropriation just bad art?

120. How do you share in and celebrate a culture without appropriating it?

121. Has FKA Twigs pulled this off in her use of vogueing?

122. Why do we appropriate cultures across not only race/nationality but also class?

123. How important is money and capitalism in discourse on cultural appropriation?

124. How important is the concept of community in cultural appropriation?

125. What is an ethical cultural exchange, what does it look like?

126. When I say 'The White Gaze' – what do you think of?

127. When I say 'Black Humanity' what do you think of?

128. When I say 'White Gaze' – what do you think I mean?

129. How do I resist 'The White Gaze'?

130. Is it even possible to resist 'The White Gaze'?

131. What does 'The White Gaze' want to see?

132. Do we make performance and assume our audiences will be white?

133. How would our work change if white was not the default?

134. What does a decolonised mind feel like?

135. What is a liberatory image of the black body?

136. Why does the phrase 'black body' slip off my tongue so easily – is this a problem?

137. Why do we share images of 'the black body'– abject, mortified, in trauma – with such ease?

138. Will I ever forget seeing: Mike Brown in the street, Tamir Rice in the park, Eric Garner in the street, Sandra Bland pulled out of her car, a police man kneeling on a 14yr of girl's back? Now that I have seen?

139. When we disseminate those images – who is our audience?

140. Why do we position problematic elements of hip-hop as exceptions to our society – rather than embodiments of the norm?

141. How do you reconcile emancipatory politics with a desire to get low/drop it like it's hot/ dutty whine?

142. Have you seen Süßer Duft? How did it make you feel?

143. Have you see Jamal Harewood's The Privileged? How did it make you feel?

144. Did you see Exhibit B? How did it make you feel?

145. Have you seen 'O' by Project O? How did it make you feel?

146. Have you ever watched Love and Hip Hop? How did that make you feel?

147. What is the relationship between gentrification and segregation?

148. What is the artist's role in gentrification?

149. Do artists have any responsibilities when it comes to gentrification?

150. Do artists have any responsibilities when interacting with' soft power'?

151. What is the relationship between artists touring internationally and imperial power?

152. How much does the race of an artist matter when we critique their work?

153. It feels like race is in fashion now. What will happen when it is not anymore?

154. Does discourse around identity encourage artists to take more risk?

155. What is the relationship between race and our ideas about expertise?

156. How do you make things more accessible without them becoming tokenistic?

157. How would you define tokenism?

158. How do you make something accessible without it being patronising?

159. How would we read Kanye West's arrogance if he was white?

160. What is the difference between a white man saying 'classism is the new racism' and a black man saying it?

161. To what extent does an artist like Kanye West makes money out of exploiting racial discourse?

162. To what extent am I doing that now?

163. Do we automatically read artists of colour as radical?

164. What expectations of authenticity do we place on artists of colour?

165. What expectations of authenticity do we place on people of colour in general?

166. Will Lupita N'yongo ever play an unlucky in love wedding planner?

167. Will a black woman ever win an Oscar without playing a maid or child molester or slave?

168. Will we ever have a black James Bond? (Would that be a good thing?)

169. If colonialism and chattel slavery had never happened, how would different cultures sit beside each other?

170. What is the cultural purpose of the stereotype of the angry black woman?

171. Who is truly silenced in our society?

172. How do we balance amplifying voices not heard without leaving all the work to the people most affected by the violence?

173. How do we balance using our voices to tell stories not told without drowning out the voices the stories belong to?

174. Why does representation matter?

175. What were The Village People trying to teach us about racial harmony?

176. What is the difference between a black performer's relationship with abjection and a white performer's?

177. To what extent did Lena Dunham need to include black characters in 'Girls' if she doesn't actually know any in her own life?

178. How should I feel about Vogue deciding that this summer is the summer of Dashiski?

179. And how should I feel about Chanel rebranding the gelling of baby hairs as 'urban curls'?

180. What the fuck do people mean when they say urban anyway?

181. How did you feel about Nicki Minaj's Anaconda Video?

182. Why do you think Miley Cyrus surrounded herself with Black Women to launch this new part of her career?

183. What do you do if you're a black person that can't dance? (Asking for a friend)

184. What do you do if you're a black person that can't sing? (Obviously not me)

185. Can we cultivate objectivity, or is it better to have a range of voices being honest about their subjectivity?

186. ...do you like watermelon?

187. Do we see twerking as sexual simply because it's something that 'black people do'?

188. What happens when an element of 'your' culture that you do not engage in is 'appropriated'?

189. What if you're not bothered by cultural appropriation but other voices in 'your community' are?

190. Why were fights in Big Brother almost always split along racial lines?

191. How do you feel about the song 'Young Gifted and Black'?

192. What was going on – in terms of consent, race and gender – when Drake was kissed by Madonna mid performance at Coachella this year?

193. When was the last time you were surrounded by artists of colour?

194. How did you feel?

195. When was the last time you were surrounded by white artists?

196. How did you feel?

197. What are the problems with the term 'of colour'?

198. Is there a relationship between CHRISTEENE and race?

199. How can I be more like Grace Jones?

200. How did you feel about the portrayal of black women in Season 2 of Orange is the New Black?

201. How do you feel about the character of Piper in Orange is the New Black?

202. How do you feel about the moments in Orange is the New Black in which black women laugh at white women?

203. Why did Bill Cosby get away with being a serial rapist for so long?

204. Why do so many people instinctively defend him?

205. Why does Black Twitter teach us about the cultural influence of people of colour?

206. Why is R. Kelly seen as the punchline to joke so often?

207. Why do we celebrate his music – which is misogynistic and predatory in nature – when he is a known paedophile and sexual predator?

208. Is it because he attacked black girls?

209. Why do we perceive blackness as 'cool'?

210. In what ways is this problematic?

211. If we frame '12 years a slave' as the third part of a trilogy on shame how does our reading of the film change?

212. Why does Kill Bill begin with murder of a Black Woman?

213. What fresh horrors will Quentin Tarantino cook up in his new film on white supremacy?

214. What is the name for the moment of dread felt just before 'nigger' is said in a rap song, when you're surrounded by white people?

215. Is it okay to rap/sing along if no one is around?

216. What does the answer to this question tell us about use of the word 'nigger' in private and public space?

217. Why is that word yet to lose its potency?

218. Why is Chris Brown's domestic violence spoken about so often, but the domestic violence of white men is hidden?

219. Where is Frank Ocean?

220. Why is Morrissey so racist?

221. Why do I love him anyways?

222. How do we reconcile the racism of people whose work we adore with their talent?

223. How do we reconcile Ghandi's disdain for black people – and his sexual abuse – with the importance of some of his teachings?

224. Why does music from Black churches have such a unique power?

225. Do I fancy Michael Fassbender because he is actually attractive – or because I know he finds black women attractive?

226. What is going on in that bit in Bride and Prejudice, when Lalita dreams of an English wedding, and is surrounded by exclusively white people, with no trace of her own culture?

227. Why does Tina Fey have such a problematic relationship with race?

228. Is art more likely to ask us to empathise with the oppressor or the oppressed?

229. How did you feel about the treatment of race in Chris Brett Bailey's 'This Is How We Die'?

230. How do you feel about Spike Lee?

231. Have you accepted Junglepussy into your life as your Lord and Saviour?

232. How would this piece be different if my race was different?

233. How would my life be different if my race was different?

234. What is it like to be white?

235. If I went on Stars in their Eyes, could I be Kate Bush?

236. When is the best time to listen to Mary J Blige – when you leave your husband or when you take him back?

237. How did Iman feel about being described as 'the best of black and the best of white?

238. Who is the greatest rapper of all time?

239. Why did Beyoncé and Jay Z model themselves after Bonnie and Clyde?

240. A billboard review described Kendrick Lamar's Christianity as 'radical' – is that even possible?

241. Why, when Azealia Banks correctly called out cultural smudging, were people quick to remind us about her use of homophobic language?

242. There is a moment in the film 'Dear White People' when a white man tells the black female protagonist that she 'longs to be oppressed' – why does this statement silence her so effectively?

243. Who is Live Aid for?

244. What is Live Aid for?

245. If you are from an African Country, living in the UK, how does Live Aid make you feel?

246. When your words exist beyond you – are taken into other contexts – what do you lose and what do you gain?

247. Who is bell hooks writing for?

248. When I say 'everyone' – who comes to mind, who do you visualise in your head?

249. We often talk about debating race – what is there to debate?

250. Toni Morrison says that James Joyce, Tchaikovsky – all the greats – were writing about race all the time – we just never read them that way. What do you think about this?

251. What is afrofuturism?

252. Why is so much of the iconography of Afrofuturism referencing Ancient Egypt?

253. Is Sun Ra a genius or terrible?

254. What (if any) are the problems with Janelle Monae's song and video for 'Yoga'?

255. What was W.E.B. Dubois referring to when he spoke of 'the double consciousness' of black folks?

256. How much power do Black Hollywood actors have to be auteurs in the roles they play?

257. What does Mohammed Ali dream about?

258. What would the TV series 'Roots' look like without all the scenes designed to make sure white people didn't feel bad?

259. Why did Blaxploitation films never really develop into something else?

260. Who's the cop that won't drop out when there's danger all about?

261. What was it like to have sex with Barry White?

262. Why was the Fresh Prince of Bel Air so popular?

263. Is who we love inherently political?

264. Why could Stanley Kubrick imagine anti gravity, artificial intelligence, and space travel in 2001: Space Odyssey – but not people of colour being around?

265. What relationship will race have with the end of the world?

266. Does Emma – my producer – feel any anxiety about producing work that deals with race so explicitly?

267. Should she?

268. Has the 'Creative Case for Diversity' worked? Can it ever?

269. At what point does an Iggy Azalea become a Rachel Dolezal?

270. When we discuss that type of cultural appropriation, where is responsibility divided between artist and record label?

271. What is the violence of silence?

272. How does 'politeness' allow us to oppress – or at least help us do it?

273. What happened to So Solid Crew?

274. Will Sisqo ever get the credit he deserves for using the full string section of an orchestra on a song about G-Strings?

275. Why did Nelly not bother to make the chorus of 'Hot in Herre' rhyme?

276. Anne Lamott has spoken about being happiest when 'surrounded by people of colour'. She is white. How does this make you feel?

277. Joni Mitchell used to black up and drag up, and go out in New York – she says that because of this, she 'knows the struggle of the black man'. How does this make you feel?

278. When I was younger, and my dad and I used to watch soaps, he would often complain that the black man weren't 'real black men'. What did he mean?

279. When we complain about 'offensive' stand up – are we censoring comics?

280. When does critique become censorship?

281. When does calling out become censorship?

282. Is self-censorship a contradiction in terms?

283. What is the difference between censorship from an institution and censorship from protestors?

284. Do protestors truly have the power to censor?

285. What does the film 'Avatar' tell us about race?

286. What does the film 'The Last Samurai' tell us about race?

287. Is race more/less of a thing in American Comedy than British Comedy?

288. What is Kim Kardashian's relationship to race?

289. ...who cares?

290. If I should work internationally, in a county that had a relationship with blackness I wasn't used to, and something painful happened – who would look after me?

291. Would my host have the tools to know what was going on?

292. If they didn't, would they listen to me, believe me – take my word for it?

293. What is it like for Emma, to watch me learn these things and see how they change me?

294. Do other artists have the tools to have these kinds of conversations with me?

295. How can I equip my community?

296. What is the place for rigorous critique in the arts?

297. What is the relationship between race as an academic discipline and race as lived experience?

298. At what point is it oppression, not just offence?

299. What are we saying when we say a piece of work had bad politics?

300. Would a black woman ever really compare her blackness to that of a cockroach?

301. Why did the Sugababes hate each other?

302. Did Zayn Malik find being in One Direction oppressive?

303. If Maya Rudolph, Rashida Jones and Adrian Piper are all black, what does that tell me about blackness?

304. Do you remember when Cheryl Cole beat up a toilet attendant and called her a 'black bitch'? It was before she married Ashley Cole.

305. The British Council used to be a part of the UK's colonial office. What does that tell me about the organisation?

306. How far do things ever truly move from their roots?

307. What are the origins of the popular Black British phrase: 'Go suck your mom'?

308. Who have I forgotten about?

309. When was the last time you watched a piece of performance, and felt like its creator couldn't see you?

310. What is the point of provocation?

311. Do you feel provoked?

312. What do you think of the film East is East?

313. What are your thoughts on the cover of Grace Jones seminal album 'Island Life'?

314. Should Beyoncé have got that VMA or Taylor Swift?

315. Should Beyoncé have got that Grammy or Beck?

316. How can artists of colour create their own definitions of success – outside of a framework that demands exceptionalism from them?

317. How can my mum and dad help me negotiate race in spaces they have no experience – the arts, academia, etc.?

318. Why did my mum work so hard to get me black Barbies when I was little?

319. How did she feel when I chose to play with the white one anyways?

320. Why did Princess Tiana have to be a frog for the majority of the film?

321. Why is there no black Disney prince?

322. If you find your daughter with a cardigan over her head, pretending she has long, flowing hair, what should you do?

323. How would Marina Abramovic's body of work be read if she was black woman?

324. Does the race of Narcissister matter?

325. How do we make sure that we don't exclude others as we have been excluded?

326. If you are a lecturer or teacher, what is your responsibility to teach the work of people of colour?

327. In my entire academic career, no one ever signposted me to black art or black artists. Why?

328. But then how would I have responded if they had?

329. Is colour-blind casting a good thing?

330. What's the most important book about race ever written?

331. Once you start to 'see race' can you ever unsee it?

332. What can the movie 'Bring It On' teach us about race?

333. If, 100 years from now, someone did this piece again, what questions would remain, and which would be obsolete?

334. Who stole all the Black Girls from Mean Girls?

335. What can the movie 'Clueless' teach us about race?

336. Does it matter that the woman who made 'Paris is Burning' is white?

337. In that movie, one of the queens – I think it's Venus Xtravaganza says that she dreams of being a 'spoilt, rich, white girl in the suburbs'. What does this tell me?

338. Would Mr Rochester have married me, or locked me in the attic?

339. Can you perform for the male gaze – and enjoy it – and still be a feminist?

340. Was bell hooks right to call Beyoncé a visual terrorist?

341. Was Angela Davis right to say this was an irresponsible use of language from bell?

342. Dre Dre has apologised to Dee Barnes, the woman he hospitalised in the 80s. Will he pay her for all the money she lost when he had her industry blacklisted?

343. What should you say when your best friend says 'I'm not sure if this is racist, but I feel like all black people can sing'?

344. Where did she get that idea from?

345. Is it morally right to take a photograph of how red she goes when you remind her of this anecdote?

346. Or would it be more fun to record a video of the two of you laughing about it?

347. What is 7/11 (a Beyoncé song) about?

348. If you were Beyoncé would you give interviews?

349. More than anything, is race about constantly being misunderstood?

350. When will this all end?

351. There was a performance at this Fringe that contained the line: 'Maybe One Day Africa will be the most important continent in the world'. Where does Africa rank currently to this company?

352. How do you define the importance of a continent?

353. Who gets to make that kind of judgement call about 1/6 of the planet?

354. Why did D'Angelo call his comeback album 'Black Messiah'?

355. How does Deray McKesson feel about finding himself a 21st century civil rights leader?

356. People threaten to kill him online. Who will help him be safe?

357. The FBI track him as a high risk threat. Who will protect him from his government?

358. Why are shows focused around women of colour more likely to be compared to telenovelas than prestige dramas?

359. How does Shonda Rimes feel about all the expectation and responsibility placed on her?

360. What kind of TV would a British Shonda Rimes makes?

361. What would this text look like if made with an Australian artist?

362. What would this text look like if a team of artists wrote it together?

363. Why do people often presume I am a spoken word artist?

364. How will travelling change my perception of blackness?

365. Will travelling change my perception of whiteness?

366. How do you respond to someone saying: "I only let Russian women do my Bikini Line'?

367. Or 'I only let Indian women shape my eyebrows'?

368. Or 'I only let women from Senegal braid my hair'?

369. Was James Baldwin happy?

370. How did the Supremes feel about the movie Dreamgirls?

371. Has Aretha Franklin always been this bitchy?

372. If we saw programming as a political act, how would that change the diversity of work programmed?

373. Wait, sorry, I've gotten a little bit ahead of myself – do we see and treat programming as a political act?

374. Is programming a political act regardless of how you frame it?

375. Someone told me once that they believe AAVE is more expressive than standard English. What do you think?

376. When we say mainstream do we mean white?

377. Why do we have so many euphemisms for the word 'white'?

378. What does it mean to have your work on display at a British Embassy?

379. Why is the work of people of colour so often erased?

380. How do I stop this happening to my work?

381. How do we read art by writers of colour?

382. What is art's relationship to power?

383. What is the relationship between art, power and race?

384. At what point can the art we create do harm?

385. Which culture makes the best fried chicken?

386. What should be on the menu for a dinner party in which we discuss race?

387. What would be the 'critical context' in which Exhibit B would not get withdrawn?

388. Sigh. Why can I not let that shit go?

389. But – What is the political power of refusing to move on?

390. 'Why don't black people smile in photographs'?

391. 'Why are black people so loud?'

392. 'Why are black children so rude? '

393. 'Why are black women so judgmental?'

394. 'Why do black people always look so angry before you talk to them?'

395. 'Why are black people so vibrant and free?'

396. 'But you're Black...why do you have an English Accent?'

397. 'Why are black people so sensitive?'

398. Why are small black girls twerking read as sexual?

399. Why is black womanhood read simultaneously as hyper sexualised and undesirable?

400. When does a desire become a fetish?

401. The last time I did Race Cards, questions about porn and sex were what people were most defensive about – why do you think that is?

402. What is the relationship between pornography and race?

403. What is the relationship between sex and race?

404. Why do dating apps allow you to set a racial preference?

405. Do you have a racial preference when dating?

406. What does it mean if you only watch porn of one race?

407. What if that race is different from your own?

408. What if that race is a race you would never want to have sex with in 'real life'?

409. Why is our culture so obsessed with the idea of the 'Big Black Cock'?

410. What is the appropriate response to being told you will not be booked, because a venue 'already has a black woman performance artist that season'?

411. What is an appropriate response to somebody putting their fingers in your afro and saying 'it's like wool, you're like a sheep!'?

412. What is an appropriate response to somebody telling you your Afro is in the way, and putting a coat over your head?

413. What is an appropriate response to somebody telling you that you 'relaxing an afro' is like her getting a curly perm in the 80s?

414. What is an appropriate response to somebody – another POC – telling you that you will have to be 'an exceptional negro' to have any kind of art career?

415. What is an appropriate response to a friend telling you about the time they were on holiday, in France, and a white man spat in their face and called them a black whore?

416. What is an appropriate response to you talking about Benedict Cumberbatch referring to POC as coloured, and a friend responding with a list of all racist pejoratives they have been called?

417. What is an appropriate response to the friend who mentions you are black every time that you meet?

418. What is an appropriate response to Black Americans telling you that Europe is a racial haven?

419. What is the appropriate response to being told 'Black people can't fall in love in Paris'?

420. What is the appropriate response to your GP saying 'We know that people from your ethnic background don't handle mental health well, so well done for coming'?

421. What is the appropriate response to other black people telling you that you are not black enough?

422. What is an appreciate response to a white person telling you that you are not black enough?

423. What is an appropriate response to an OKCupid conversation opening with the words 'Hey Chocolate Mama!'?

424. What is an appropriate response to somebody asking to call you 'a nigger' in bed?

425. What is an appropriate response to being asked to call someone else 'a nigger' in bed?

426. What is an appropriate response to somebody calling a friend post sex to let that friend know that they 'Just fucked a black girl'?

427. What is an appropriate response to overhearing a conversation in which people compare the taste of 'pussy from around the globe'?

428. What is an appropriate response to someone telling you 'It's not that they won't date black girls, more that they're never found one attractive'?

429. What is an appropriate response to being told that you are lucky to be black?

430. What is the appropriate response to being told that whatever the Blacks have suffered, the Jews have had it worse?

431. What is an appropriate response to being called a black supremacist?

432. What is an appropriate response to being told that someone 'can't really imagine a black lesbian'?

433. What is an appropriate response to your work – which has nothing to do with black history – being advertised as part of black history month without your consent?

434. Last one for a little while: What is an appropriate response to telling a friend this, and them responding: 'If you're going to be that kind of artist now, I don't think it's a big deal'?

435. What did she mean when she said 'that kind of artist'?

436. When somebody tells me I am playing the race card, what are they really telling me?

437. When this happens, what is my appropriate response?

438. What is an appropriate response to my mum telling me she strategically gave me a name that didn't sound too black?

439. What is an appropriate response to your daughter calling you in tears because she just saw a racist show, but she couldn't leave because she knows too many people in the audience?

440. What is an appropriate response to your father saying: 'You know this is what white people are like. Take a deep breath, stop crying and go back in there'?

441. What is an appropriate response to your mother telling you that if you talk about race you'll ruin everything?

442. What is an appropriate response to an Artistic Director saying to you 'the fact of the matter is, most BAME artists make terrible work – how can we help them?' ?

443. What is an appropriate response to a programmer telling you that 'black audiences make white audiences feel uncomfortable.'?

444. What is an appropriate response to a programmer telling you that 'black audiences only support black work so aren't worth investing in'?

445. What is an appropriate response to Caitlyn Jenner saying that Serena Williams 'looks like more of a man than I ever did'?

446. What is an appropriate response to somebody comparing a show about race to a show about albinism?

447. What is an appropriate response to being called 'a coon'?

448. What is an appropriate response to Blackface in British Comedy? (Mighty Boosh, Little Britain etc.)

449. What is an appropriate response to somebody telling you that the fact you used to work at KFC is 'the blackest thing they've ever heard'?

450. Have you ever stopped yourself from eating something for fear of being a stereotype?

451. What is an appropriate response to a programmer wanting to put an artist's work about race in the natural history museum?

452. Have you ever stopped yourself doing anything for fear of becoming a stereotype?

453. What is an appropriate response to a friend introducing you thusly: 'This is Selina – Shaniqua when she's mad'?

454. What is the relationship between agency and race?

455. What is an appropriate response to contestants on RuPaul's Drag Race stuffing/padding their arses to a grotesque extent in a 'ghetto booty' challenge, then twerking across the room?

456. What is an appropriate response to being told that black women don't get cancer?

457. What is an appropriate response to being asked if your hair gets wet?

458. When somebody asks me where I am really from, what are they really asking me?

459. What is my appropriate response to that question?

460. What is an appropriate response to a rash going undiagnosed/diagnosed incorrectly for 6 months, and the doctor saying 'I'm so sorry – it's difficult to differentiate on black skin'?

461. What is an appropriate response to a teacher saying 'I don't know why the black girls behave worse – but they do. It's not my job to figure it out, it's my job to deal with it'?

462. What is an appropriate response to somebody saying: 'You didn't sound Black on the phone'?

463. What happens to a child in school if her teacher is 'uncomfortable talking to black parents' – so doesn't alert the child's parents to any struggles that child is having in class?

464. What is an appropriate response to this teacher asserting that she is not racist?

465. What is an appropriate response to CAKESDAKILLA saying Queerness is 'some white university bullshit'?

466. What is an appropriate response to an article on Hurricane Katrina that argues that 'the food in New Orleans has never been better' and focuses on that alone?

467. What is gained by proving Beyoncé is not a feminist?

468. What is an appropriate response to reading the 643,468th think piece on this question?

469. What is an appropriate response to Morgan Freeman saying that the way to deal with race is to stop talking about it?

470. What is an appropriate response to me noticing (and saying) that 'white men are dominating the conversation!' and ruining your event?

471. What is an appropriate response to Piers Morgan writing in the Daily Mail about black people using the word 'nigger'?

472. What is an appropriate response to Piers Morgan?

473. What is an appropriate response to somebody joking about R Kelly 'pissing on' 3-year-old Blue Ivy?

474. What is an appropriate response to bell hooks telling Laverne Cox and Janet Mock that how they wear their hair reinforces Eurocentric patriarchal beauty ideas?

475. What is an appropriate response to bell hooks writing in 'Outlaw Culture' that 'RuPaul is a Big Black Man trying to be a Tiny White Woman'?

476. What is an appropriate response to somebody telling you they want to have children of a specific race in order for that child to have desired characteristics?

477. What is the appropriate response to a review of Summertime '06 in which Vince Staples is descried as a 'brute'?

478. What is an appropriate response to Benefit saying they can't make darker skin make up because it's too difficult to get right?

479. What is an appropriate response to somebody remarking every time they come to your house that your neighbourhood is 'rough'?

480. Do you remember the time Lily Allen tweeted a pic of her boyfriend's cock dressed up as Gollywog?

481. What is an appropriate response to Gollywog dolls?

482. Have you spotted the Blackamoor figurine in Drill Hall yet?

483. What is an appropriate response to art that uses the figure of the Blackamoor?

484. What is an appropriate response to people who think 'interracial love' is the only way to end racism?

485. What is an appropriate response to Mad Max Fury Road having only one black woman in it – and her being plugged up to a milking machine like an animal?

486. What is an appropriate response to somebody saying 'we're all just human'?

487. What is an appropriate response to being told 'I speak surprisingly well' by somebody who has just met me?

488. What is an appropriate response to being called 'Brown Sugar' in the street?

489. What is an appropriate response to somebody seeing police brutality in the States, and saying to me 'God – you must be so grateful you live here!'?

490. What is an appropriate response to the fear and panic those events inspire?

491. What is an appropriate response to somebody asking you: 'Why the fuck can't you make cornbread?'

492. What is an appropriate response to walking into a pub and seeing a woman nudge her husband and say 'look Mark, it's one of them'?

493. What is an appropriate response to a 3 year old pointing at you and saying 'look Mummy, a nigger!'?

494. Why didn't 'mummy' do or say anything?

495. Why do we expect ourselves and each other to be able to deal with those moments instantly when actually they cause huge amounts of shock?

496. What is an appropriate response to a girl splitting up with her partner and her saying it was because 'he was a typical Asian man'?

497. What should you do when everybody laughs at that statement?

498. What is an appropriate response to your daughter telling you she can't go to her best friend's house because 'Mrs Ismail doesn't want Sara to be friends with a black girl'?

499. How do you explain this to your daughter?

500. How should Sara and I negotiate this story now we are adults?

501. What is an appropriate response to Perez Hilton saying he 'has a strong black woman inside of him'?

502. What is an appropriate response to somebody telling you that 'they had to be careful in India because they hate white women there'?

503. What is an appropriate response to somebody writing a blog about how happy she is in Goa because 'they love white women here'?

504. What is an appropriate response to my biracial friend tells me that the hardest thing about being in Jamaica was being privileged because of having non afro hair, light skin and green eyes?

505. What is an appropriate response to a lecture in which a Black American woman says how surprised she is that women in Ghana 'wear weaves too'?

506. What is an appropriate response to an advert for skin lightening cream on the back of a bus?

507. What would an appropriate remembrance of colonialism look like?

508. What is an appropriate response to a taxi driver from the Ivory Coast who has lived in 16 different countries telling me there is no home for him anywhere?

509. How do I answer him, when he asks me why some people see it's him driving the taxi and then stop hailing it?

510. How do I comfort him, when he tells me the story of his mother in law who never forgave her daughter for marrying a black man, and despises him?

511. What advice do I offer him when he tells me about the wife who cannot understand his grief?

512. How, in a 40 minute taxi journey can I stop him from absorbing all the poison that surrounds him?

513. What is the line – I can't carry his grief, but he can't bear it anymore, how do we negotiate that?

514. Where is that man now, is he OK?

515. How devastated must that man have been, to tell all that to the first other black person to get in his taxi?

516. How do I reconcile that conversation with reading an article in the guardian that morning about how multiculturalism has 'saved' London?

517. How much pain and anger can on person carry?

518. What happens when you are at your limit?

519. What comes after that pain and anger?

520. Are the pain and the anger one thing?

521. What does healing look like for a person of colour?

522. Sometimes people emigrate from the Caribbean or Africa, leaving a child with an Aunt. Sometimes it is years before their child can join them. What does this do to their parent-child relationship?

523. When the child finally emigrates how does the Aunt feel?

524. How do all involved parties heal from that?

525. What does healing look like for my nan?

526. Is it a return to Montserrat?

527. How does my nan feel, when she returns to the island she left over 60 years ago?

528. If she is buried there – as she would like to be, who will look after her grave? All her family are here.

529. What if she cannot be buried there?

530. What if she dies here, and My Great Uncle Paddy is left 'alone, on this miserable island none of us were meant to die on'?

531. What did freedom feel like?

533. What will freedom feel like?

Andy Field

Andy is a theatremaker, curator, and co-director of the performance collective Forest Fringe. He has toured his own contemporary performance work across the UK and internationally. Andy also writes on performance and in 2012 completed a PhD imagining new relationships with the New York avant-gardes of the 1960s.

www.andytfield.co.uk

——

Ira Brand

Ira is an artist, performance-maker and writer. She works across theatre and live art, creating live performances that are rooted in a fascination with what it means and feels like to be human. Her shows are visceral, funny and tender attempts to explore often vast contemporary topics in a way that celebrates both personal and collective experience. Ira regularly works in collaboration with other companies and artists, most recently Made In China (Gym Party) and Andy Field (put your sweet hand in mine). She co-runs Forest Fringe with Andy Field and Deborah Pearson.

——

Deborah Pearson

Deborah is an award-winning writer, performer and producer, originally from Canada and based in the UK. She regularly tours internationally, having performed her work in ten countries and on three continents. She is founder and one of the co-directors of Forest Fringe, an artist-led venue at the Edinburgh Festival that prioritises experimental work. In 2016, along with her co-directors Andy Field and Ira Brand, she was listed on the Stage 100 list of the most influential people in UK theatre. She is waiting to defend a PhD on narrative in contemporary performance at Royal Holloway, where she was a Reid Scholar and taught courses on writing for performance, devising and text in theatre.

——

Lyn Gardner

Lyn was a founder member of the City Limits co-operative. She now writes about theatre for *The Guardian* and writes children's books for Nosy Crow. Her latest book for 8 to 12 year olds, *Rose Campion and the Stolen Secret*, has just been published.

———

Action Hero

Gemma Paintin and James Stenhouse live in Bristol, UK, and create interdisciplinary performances together under the name Action Hero. For the past decade, they have worked almost exclusively with each other and have toured together to more than twenty countries across 5 continents to critical and popular acclaim. Gemma & James have been shortlisted for several awards and won an Austin (Texas) Critic's Table Award in 2013 for *Watch Me Fall*. In 2015, a book of six of their works was published by Oberon.

———

David Overend

David is a director and Lecturer in Drama and Theatre at Royal Holloway, University of London. He trained at RADA and was Associate Artist at the Arches arts centre in Glasgow (2007-2010). Directing credits include *CauseWay* by Victoria Bianchi (National Trust for Scotland); *Wallace* by Rob Drummond (the Arches and the National Theatre of Great Britain); *Marco Pantani: The Pirate* by Stuart Hepburn (Òran Mór); and *Bullet Catch* by Rob Drummond (the Arches).

davidoverend.net

———

Chris Thorpe

Chris is a writer and performer from Manchester.

———

Lucy Ellinson

Lucy is an actor and theatre maker specialising in devised and experimental performance and international new writing. Lucy is an associate artist with London's Gate Theatre and is a member of Third Angel, Deaf and Hearing Ensemble and is a core artist with Forest Fringe. Lucy has been supported by Battersea Arts Centre and regularly collaborates with artists: Chris Goode, Chris Thorpe, Clare Duffy, Unlimited Theatre, Wendy Hubbard, Metis Arts, Jane Packman Company and Lydia Ziemke/Suite42.

Tania El Khoury

Tania is an artist working between London and Beirut. She creates interactive installations and challenging performances in which the audience is an active collaborator. Tania's solo work has toured internationally, and for which she is the recipient of the Total Theatre Innovation Award and the Arches Brick Award. She is co-founder of Dictaphone Group, a research and performance collective aiming at questioning our right to the city and its public space.

Gemma Brockis

Gemma is a writer and performer and one of the founding members of the London-based performance collective SHUNT.

Sam Halmarack

Sam Halmarack and The Miserablites has been touring internationally since 2011, including performances with Forest Fringe in San Francisco in 2012 and as one of the headline acts at Melbourne Arts House Festival of Live Arts in 2014. Sam is currently making two large-scale music productions: a devised musical called Always and Totally Forever which aims to get an adult audience to feel like teenagers. He is working on a community-based spectacle *We Are Lightning!* a collaboration with Melbourne artist JOF that looks at how music shapes peoples lives and brings people together.

——

Selina Thompson

Selina is an artist and performer based in Birmingham. She makes performance and installations about identity, how it shapes our lives, politics and environments, and its relationship to freedom. Her work tends to be intimate, urgent and playful, with a taste for endurance and spectacle. In the past few years she has built dresses out of cake, 'igloos' out of hair extensions, and retraced the Transatlantic Slave route via cargo freighter. She has shown work at Spill, Fierce, Mayfest, the Birmingham REP and the West Yorkshire Playhouse.

——

Forest Fringe would like to thank all the contributors to this book.

Forest Fringe's presence in Edinburgh over the last 10 years would not have been possible without the generosity and enthusiasm of the Forest Café, Out of the Blue Drill Hall, Jerwood Charitable Foundation, Battersea Arts Centre, Queen's University Ontario, Alfred and Isabel Bader, the Department of Theatre at the University of Chichester, Ellie Dubois, Maria Moore, Alex Fernandes, James Baster, Rebecca Thomson, Will Brady, Ryan Van Winkle, Abigail Conway, Brian Lobel, Gemma Paintin, James Stenhouse, Jo Bannon, Richard DeDomenici, Tania El Khoury and all the artists, volunteers and audiences who have made it what it is.

Andy, Deborah and Ira would like to thank Maria Bako, Calum Brooks, Beckie Darlington, Ann Dewar, Shelley Hastings, Daniel K, Morgan McBride, Laura McDermott, Mary, Alan and David Pearson and Warwick Symes for all their support and advice over the last ten years.

First published in 2016 by Oberon Books Ltd
521 Caledonian Road, London N7 9RH
Tel: +44 (0) 20 7607 3637 / Fax: +44 (0) 20 7607 3629
e-mail: info@oberonbooks.com
www.oberonbooks.com

A catalogue record for this book is available from the British Library.

PB ISBN: 9781783197514

Designed by Konstantinos Vasdekis

Printed and bound in the UK

Visit www.oberonbooks.com to read more about all our books and to buy them. You will also find features, author interviews and news of any author events, and you can sign up for e-newsletters so that you're always first to hear about our new releases.

WWW.OBERONBOOKS.COM

Follow us on www.twitter.com/@oberonbooks
& www.facebook.com/OberonBooksLondon